Las Vegas
The Mob Years

STORIES OF BOOTLEGGERS, REVENGE AND MURDER

Celebrity portraits by David Tomasovsky

SCOTLINE
SL
PRESS

D'Iberville, Mississippi

For information on other books by Andrew J. McLean, visit
his web site at
www.andrewjamesmclean.com

ISBN-10: 0-9658499-9-6

ISBN-13: 978-0-9658499-9-9

CONTENTS

THE NEED FOR SELF PRESERVATION

DALITZ'S LATER YEARS

HOFFA'S EARLY LIFE

THE HOFFA /DALITZ ALLIANCE

HOFFA IN PRISON

HOFFA'S KILLER REVEALED

THE MEETING IN DETROIT

EARLY LIFE

THE OUTFIT

ACCARDO AND THE RIVIERA

EARLY LIFE

REPUTED CIA CONNECTIONS

JOHN "MARSHALL" CAIFANO

INTRODUCTION

*L*as Vegas was the American Dream: a treasure trove gangster style. During its heyday, from roughly 1950 to about 1980, The Mob was skimming an estimated $1 million a day from casino count rooms. Every week, a courier with a suitcase full of skimmed cash traveled by train to fill Mob coffers back east in places such as Kansas City, Chicago, Milwaukee, and Miami.

Meanwhile, the multi-million pension fund loans to finance Mob-run casinos kept coming, as were the loan kick backs to Jimmy Hoffa, the Teamster's General President and a Vegas visionary. Just as The Mob controlled Hoffa, they controlled an endless stream of capital to build their temples of money. By the late 1950s, no Mob in America could resist the lure of Las Vegas. They really had it good —skimming profits from a city, especially one with no law enforcement to get in their way.

In 1957, at the pinnacle of The Mob's heyday, the Tropicana opened and instantly became the most glamorous resort-hotel in town. It was modeled after tropical Mob-owned casinos in Havana, and it featured an 18-hole golf course. Shortly after the Tropicana's opening, The Mob's influence over Sin City casinos was inadvertently exposed when Frank Costello, one of America's most notorious gangsters, was shot by a rival gang member outside his New York apartment. The injury was minor, but while Costello recovered in the hospital police discovered an interesting note in his pocket. Written on it was a list detailing cash amounts from the Tropicana to be distributed to known organized crime figures. For the first time, there was finally proof that The Mob was skimming in Vegas; [1]however, the government showed little concern. It didn't interest New York cops nor the FBI. At that time, they were busy fighting communism.

Then in the mid 1960s, The Mob sent Frank Rosenthal to Vegas to run their casinos and later, sent his old pal Tony Spilotro as the overseer. Rosenthal had the smarts and provided the skim, while Spilotro made sure The Mob got their weekly suitcases full of millions in skimmed cash. But with Rosenthal's obsession with running the town—and Spilotro's penchant for breaking the rules, it finally all came tumbling down.

Years before, the syndicate bosses who ruled Sin City came to the conclusion that doing business profitably in Las Vegas required certain rules. Business could not be conducted the old fashioned way. During Prohibition, territories were divided up among gangs with the help of machine guns and dynamite. Violence wouldn't work in a city that had come to thrive on gambling tourists. If The Mob was to flourish, the dapper gaming aficionados in their high- desert refuge had to get along, maintain a low profile, and stay out of the spotlight. Gang war and bloodshed were taboo, to keep Las Vegas from being labeled as nothing more than a killing field and a city of nefarious gambling joints.

To secure the city's image, The Mob bosses mandated that contract murders must be performed outside of Nevada, thereby avoiding heat from law enforcement. Thus, when the decision was made to eliminate the Flamingo's Ben Siegel in June 1947 and the Riviera's Gus Greenbaum in December 1958, the killings occurred elsewhere.

These syndicate rules among owners became obsolete when the Chicago Outfit sent Tony Spilotro as the overseer to reassert its authoritarian rule over the street rackets. Within weeks, the discovery of five dead bodies—ex-loan sharks, beaten with their throats slashed—in the desert outside Vegas, instigated the bloody era in Sin City. That kind of action was precisely what the city's founding fathers had feared. High-profile violence inevitably led to exposure of the casino skim and the fall from grace of the traditional Mob in casino front offices.

* * *

Chapter 1

BENNY BINION: EX-DALLAS MOB BOSS MOVES TO LAS VEGAS

*J*ust prior to beginnings of The Mob's heyday in Vegas, an ex-Dallas Mob boss named Benny Binion pulled up stakes in 1947, moved his family to Las Vegas, and forever changed the style of gambling in America. The life and times of the storied Binion family, their move to Glitter

Gulch and how they built the city's most profitable casino, reads like a captivating crime saga that's hard to put down. It begins with an intriguing story of a blood feud between Benny and his ex-business partner Herbert Noble: a murderous feud that ended with two dead bodies, and another serving five years in prison.

By the summer of 1949, the ongoing Noble/Binion blood feud had endured more than a year with Herbert Noble surviving nine attempts on his life. Until then, the failed assaults were orchestrated by gunmen in drive-by shootings, but the state of affairs had changed considerably: the bounty on Noble's head doubled from $25,000 to $50,000, a prize that was rumored to lure a professional trio of killers to North Texas to finish the job.

While Benny Binion was grappling with problems at his Horseshoe Club in Las Vegas, the tenth attempt on Herbert Noble's life came in the form of a car bomb the morning of November 29, 1949. Instead of Noble, it killed his wife Mildred and instigated a vendetta that would fester for 16 long months. Later, when detectives questioned Noble about possible suspects in the crime, he refused to mention any names. Nevertheless, with an evil glare in his eyes, Noble could only speak of an ex-Dallas gambling boss who lived 1,500 miles away in Las Vegas.

PRELUDE TO A BLOOD FEUD

"In 1977 the Feds figured they had Sheriff Ralph Lamb

nailed. However, U.S. District Judge Roger D. Foley acquitted Lamb of all charges. He said the IRS had failed to prove that anybody paid for the building materials, so they probably were gifts, not subject to taxation. The acquittal came after Horseshoe Casino owner tough Benny Binion, ex-Dallas Mob boss, came forward and swore under oath, that the $30,000 in question was not a gift, but an unsecured promissory note underwritten by the Binion family." [1]

— A.D. Hopkins of the *Las Vegas Review-Journal*

Benny Binion always knew how to take care of his friends, especially those in high places. Since 1936, when local newspapers referred to Benny as the Dallas "kingpin" of underworld gambling he had maintained connections with key Dallas politicians. That was also the year Benny earned the title "boss gambler," a moniker the road gamblers, hustlers, and racketeers who continually drifted in and out of town knew him by. Benny had started in the 1920s, working as a street corner bootlegger, under the guise of a newspaper boy, until he "had charmed, bribed, and shot his way to the top of the Dallas underworld."[2]

A.D. Hopkins of the *Las Vegas Review-Journal* described one of the reasons for Binion's success. "Even in the Depression, Dallas was flush with oil money. During World War II, entire divisions of GIs learned to shoot craps in barracks and motor pools, and many headed for Dallas to buck the bigger banks and honest dice Binion was known to provide."[3]

In the waning years of his life, Benny maintained an office

13

downstairs near the entrance to the Sombrero Room Café and liked to pass the time with whoever might happen by. When Benny wasn't in his office he could usually be found in the Sombrero Room sitting in "his" big leather booth in the back corner drinking coffee. Technically, only Benny or his invited guests sat at that particular leather booth, because he owned it. For that matter, Benny owned the whole place—the hotel, the casino, and the downstairs café. Hell, the huge neon sign out front on Fremont Street said so: "'Binion's Horseshoe Club' flashed in giant gold neon letters on a block-long blue neon background. The hundred dollar chips in the casino had his picture on them. Even the specialty of the house in the Sombrero Room was named after him. 'Benny Binion's Jailhouse Chili' they called it."[4]

From 1947 to 1953, Benny owned and operated Binion's Horseshoe Club, which almost from the day it opened was the most profitable casino in Las Vegas. But after a 1953 felony conviction for income tax evasion, he was prohibited from holding a Nevada gaming license. From then on Benny's two sons ran the downtown Horseshoe—the elder Jack Binion as president, and Ted Binion as casino manager. In 1958, after completing a five-year term of incarceration, Benny worked as the Horseshoe's consultant out of his downstairs office.

But even a stretch in Leavenworth Penitentiary couldn't stop Benny from coming down to the Horseshoe's coffee shop "dressed in his big Stetson hat, his cowboy shirt with the buttons made from three-dollar gold pieces, and his ostrich boots."[5] And it surely didn't keep him from talking about gambling, rodeos, his days in Dallas, or just about any subject a person may care to talk about.

Benny would tell the story about the "suitcase man," William Lee Bergstrom, a Texas gambler who wanted to try his luck and risk it all on one throw of the dice. In the early 1980s Bergstrom decided to test the claim that Binion's Horseshoe would book any bet, no matter how large, as long it was the first wager a player made. Bergstrom arrived at the Horseshoe with a suitcase filled with money and said he wanted to bet the entire amount on the Don't Pass Line at craps. A casino supervisor took the suitcase to the cashier's cage, where the amount was verified at $777,000. The suitcase full of money was physically placed on the Don't Pass Line. The shooter, a lady, came out with a roll of six then sevened out two rolls later. A casino supervisor counted out $777,000 in casino cheques, Bergstrom picked up the winning cheques along with the suitcase full of cash, cashed in at the casino cashier, and departed.

Or Benny might talk about the fabled poker game of 1949 between Nick "the Greek" Dandalos and Johnny Moss. "Spread the game for 'em right out there in front of the casino. Damn game went on for almost four months. I think Johnny won about $400,000." [6] Interestingly, the 42-year-old Moss had to rest by taking naps on a regular basis. During the naps, Nick the Greek, then 57, passed his time playing craps. After months of playing heads-up poker and seeing his opponent, Johnny Moss, win a small fortune, Dandalos uttered one of the most famous poker statements of all time: "Mister Moss, I have to let you go."[7]

Yet, most of all Benny loved to talk about his days in Dallas, about the high times of running wide open. He loved the stories of bootleggers, of cow punchin' and gamblers, and when he felt up to it, he would tell stories about the Prohibition days in Dallas.

All you had to do was ask, as did a reporter from the *Houston Chronicles* who once asked Benny in an interview about his early days in North Texas. "Yessir, I can damn sure tell you about Dallas. I'll tell you the truth, too."[8] And then a big smile would shine across his weathered face, and he would laugh. "I'll tell you the truth, but I ain't gonna tell you everything."[9]

THE INNOVATOR WHO PUSHED THE LIMITS

A.D. Hopkins said it well when he described the innovative Benny Binion: "He was a cowboy who pushed the limits. A Texan who knew a thing or two about horse trading, and gambling, and laid his claim on Fremont Street, and changed the face of Western hospitality."[10]

Born the son of a North Texas horse trader on November 20, 1904, near the tiny community of Pilot Grove in Grayson County, about 50 miles north of Dallas, Benny spent much of his early years traveling with his father around the Panhandle region. Because of his poor health—by the age of ten he was stricken with pneumonia on at least four occasions—his parents kept him out of school, thinking the boy would benefit from being in the open air. Benny learned to gamble with traders who gathered with his father at the various campgrounds near western rodeos and other popular events where horses were bought and sold, such as county fairs.

Benny became fascinated with the gambling and the gamblers, and took particular interest in the dice games, which he watched carefully and learned. During those days when he traveled with his father, the horse traders and road gamblers played "money craps" as opposed to "bank craps," the casino game played today on complex layouts with three croupiers, and a box man watching over the game protecting a bank of $500,000 or more. In money craps, the "shooter" announces the amount of money he wants to wager. Other players in the game have the option to cover (or "fade") all or any portion of the wager. Should the other players not fade the entire wager, the shooter has the option of rolling the dice for the amount the faders have agreed to wager, or pass the dice to the next shooter. Proposition bets between players are permitted, such as the shooter making his point of ten the "hard way"—rolling 5-5, versus rolling 6-4 or 4-6, which in casino parlance is called the "easy way." Players in money craps are also permitted to wager each other for or against the shooter.

Benny lived the life of a nomadic horse trader until, at the age of 16, he decided to go out on his own. In Binion's biography, *I'll Do My Own Damn Killin'*, author Gary W. Sleeper describes Benny in those days. "Photos taken on his sixteenth birthday depict a full-grown, robust young man, round-faced and smiling under his newsboy's cap, standing about six feet tall and weighing about 190 pounds."[11]

For the next six years Benny traveled across most of Texas, though he spent most of his time in El Paso, described as a wild-and-woolly frontier town. When Prohibition became the law of the land in 1919, a large-scale whiskey smuggling business developed along the Mexican border across the Rio Grande. And most likely Benny earned much of his income transporting unlawful spirits from Mexico into El Paso.

The usually talkative Benny, who at the drop of a hat could overflow, jawing about his life in Texas, became unusually quiet when queries were made about his days in El Paso. In his waning years, months before his death Benny was asked by a newspaper reporter about his days in El Paso. "I got to be known pretty fast," he said. How? "Well, I wouldn't want to tell it."[12]

For whatever reason, by 1922 Benny had enough of El Paso and relocated to Dallas and immediately took up bootlegging. Under the pretext of a newspaper boy, Benny sold bootleg whiskey on downtown street corners with two young men who would evolve as his life-long friends: Chill Wills, the acclaimed Hollywood character actor and Johnny Moss, one of the world's greatest tournament poker players. In a 1989 interview with Steven R. Reed of the *Houston Chronicles*, Benny described those days:

> *I bootlegged in and out of town. I'd leave and come back. In and out.   I'd leave town and go out and punch cows, trade horses, do something like that, then come back. Never made no money in nothing. Started making money from about '26.*[13]

THE GROWTH OF DALLAS

By the early 1930s, Dallas owed its fortune to the production of two commodities—cotton and crude oil. The city is located at the convergence of two railroads, which in the late 1800s made it a natural shipping center for the cotton produced throughout central and northern Texas, and by the turn of the century Dallas had become the world's largest cotton market.

In 1930, Dallas would also witness the beginning of a sizable oil boom. As luck would have it, a 70-year old wildcatter named Columbus Marion "Dad" Joiner "convinced that he could locate oil in East Texas, began drilling in Rusk County about 50 miles east of Dallas. After two dry holes, Joiner drilled one last well on the spot where his truck had broken down. This third well, the one he called the Daisy Bradford #3, became the first find in the huge East Texas field, the largest in the world at the time."[14] Soon a myriad of oil derricks spotted the East Texas plains.

While Texas, along with the rest of America, suffered in the grips of the Great Depression during the 1930s, Dallas prospered. The oil fields brought jobs for roughnecks, pipe fitters, truck drivers, mechanics and tool pushers, all spending their paychecks in Dallas. As the money flowed, oil-related businesses began springing up around the city. Contractors, equipment suppliers, and speculators all found Dallas, as well as the established oil fields in Beaumont and neighboring Louisiana, a convenient location for a base of operations.

By 1933, the petroleum industry had supplanted the cotton market as the lifeblood of the Dallas economy, and the city's population swelled to more than 250,000 residents, practically doubling in ten years. About this time the city was also aided by the completion of a mammoth project redirecting the Trinity River channel, which finally relieved the threat of constant flooding.

BENNY'S EARLY DAYS IN NORTH TEXAS

In his younger days as a bootlegger in North Texas, Benny carried three pistols—two .45 automatics holstered under each shoulder and a small .38 revolver in his coat pocket. When Benny developed underworld gambling in Dallas, the ocean of money he made attracted ruthless pirates. There was a rumor that, for whatever reason, when Benny had to kill someone he'd shoot his victim with a .45 and then use the .38 to shoot himself inflicting a nonfatal wound, for instance in the fleshy upper arm. Allegedly, Benny would then place the .38 near the body to make it appear the victim had shot at him. It was also rumored that later, when Benny surrendered to police, he'd claim self defense, stating that the dead man had shot first.

In 1931, Benny suspected fellow bootlegger Frank Bolding of hijacking a truckload of his liquor. He confronted Bolding, who according to Ted Binion "was a real bad man, [and] had a reputation for killing people by stabbing them." In one confrontation, Bolding "stood up real quick and Dad felt like he was going to stab him," so Binion "rolled back pulled his gun, and shot upward from the ground. Hit him through the neck and killed him."[15] The incident earned Benny his nickname "The Cowboy." It also earned him a murder conviction. During the investigation, authorities discovered Bolding had a knife but hadn't pulled it. Nevertheless, Benny received only a two-year suspended sentence, because Bolding's reputation was so bad.

By 1936, Benny had become the reigning Mob boss of Dallas. Soon, after he tried to muscle in on the gambling rackets in nearby Fort Worth, The Mob boss of that city, Lewis Tindell was found dead.

On September 12, 1936, Benny Binion cruised through North Dallas in his Cadillac with Buddy Malone at the wheel. Malone was a chief lieutenant in Benny's lucrative policy business, a numbers racket that was the bread and butter of his underworld gambling empire earning him $1 million annually. That Saturday afternoon Benny and Malone drove toward the Pride of Dallas Café, a popular establishment in the predominantly African-American part of town, intending to survey the action in their territory.

When they turned north onto Allen Street, Benny spotted Ben Frieden sitting in a car parked at the curb in front of the café. Frieden was a 46-year-old bookmaker and gambler, who had come to Dallas from California at the onset of the oil boom. Frieden operated a produce business in the Dallas public market, but had recently started a small but expanding policy game in North Dallas. Benny didn't take kindly to interlopers moving in on his business, and Frieden's so-called top-notch policy wheel had not escaped the boss gambler's attention, so Benny had warned the intruder to find another city for his policy racket, preferably in another state.

When Benny spotted his competitor conducting business out in the open, he became furious. Benny, whose tough reputation was already legendary in Dallas, especially after killing Frank Bolding five years earlier, yelled at Malone to stop the car. The cowboy threw the Cadillac's door open, "and ran to the passenger side of Frieden's automobile. Reaching through the open window, he slapped Frieden across the face."

Binion then screamed, "You son of a bitch, you're a sucker in the business. You don't know no better and I'm gonna forgive you this time. But don't come around here again or I'll whip your ass."

"You might do it," Frieden replied, "but you won't do it today."[16]

What happened next is not entirely clear. The version told by Binion and Malone stated that Frieden pulled a pistol and shot at Binion, with the bullet hitting him in the right arm. Binion went for his shoulder holster grabbed his .45 and shot Frieden in the heart.

At the sound of gun fire, Malone leapt from his boss's car and simultaneously pulled out his own .45 automatic and began shooting through the driver's side window. Benny would later tell an interviewer, "Old Buddy just shot the piss out of him."[17]

During the gunfight Frieden's chauffeur, George Parker, somehow eluded the bullets aimed at Frieden. He escaped from the melee relatively unharmed but nearly deafened, and was so traumatized that he was incapable of making a statement to detectives.

Benny and Malone climbed back in the Cadillac and drove away. Minutes later, when the police arrived on the scene, they found Parker clutching the wheel so severely shaken that he was incoherent. They also found Frieden dead, with six bullet wounds in his chest and back. Lying on the seat next to his body was a .38 revolver containing one spent cartridge.

Three hours later, Benny surrendered to authorities for the killing of Frieden. Two days passed before Malone turned himself in and confirmed Benny's version of the story—that Frieden had shot first and Benny had fired in self defense.

Nevertheless, investigators found witnesses who claimed they saw Benny toss an object into Frieden's car after the gunfight, which conjured up worries that the .38 revolver found next to Frieden's body had been Binion's. Benny and Malone were indicted, but three months later the judge dismissed the indictments based on lack of evidence.

By 1936, with protection from the police and local politicians, Benny had gained control of gambling operations in Dallas. At the time, the local FBI office already had an extensive open file on Benny Binion which included mentions of occasional contacts with wise guys in the Eastern Mob, including Meyer Lansky, as well as connections to the Chicago Outfit.

By the end of World War II, more than 24 "casinos" operated illegally in downtown Dallas hotels, and Benny Binion owned at least half of them. But it was Benny's numbers racket that gave him most of his wealth, over $1 million annually, and he didn't like competitors moving in on his bread and butter. But an ambitious ex-partner of Benny's named Herbert Noble had dreams of being a gambling boss, and when Sam Murray was killed Noble quickly became the cowboy's only true rival for gambling supremacy in Dallas.

THE RISE OF HERBERT NOBLE

Herbert Noble was born in April 1909, 80 miles west of Fort Worth, and by his ninth birthday his family had settled in West Dallas. Technically, West Dallas did not exist. The impoverished creation is described by author Gary Sleeper: "The bastard stepchild of the city of Dallas, it hunkered down on the west bank of the Trinity, almost in the shadows of the downtown skyscrapers."[18] Most of the residents lived in shacks they built from materials scavenged from the dump nearby. The upscale poor of West Dallas owned or rented dilapidated shacks that had been wheeled over the river from Dallas and put down wherever a flat, and hopefully elevated, parcel of land could be found. Essentially, it was an unincorporated slum with no zoning, hardly any running water, and one paved street named Eagle Ford Road. When it rained the Trinity River often overflowed its banks and swamped the area, leaving the ramshackle housing in ruin and the dirt roads a muddy mess.

In 1919, part of a wave of resettlement from destitute nearby farms, the Barrow family, including Henry, his wife Cumie and seven children, relocated to the nearby urban slum known as West Dallas. When the Barrows arrived they lived under the wagon brought with them, until Henry saved enough money to purchase a tent. By 1920, Barrow worked at a general store and gas station, about a mile west of the Trinity, selling five-cent bottles of Coca Cola, Bull Durham tobacco, and drinking water in five gallon casks. His boys—Clyde, Buck, LC and Jack—frequently ran afoul of the law, especially Clyde, who during a recent term of incarceration killed an inmate that had sexually assaulted him. Clyde was paroled in February 1932 from Eastham Prison Farm, and after his release took up with a petite redhead named Bonnie Parker. Together as part of the notorious Barrow gang, Bonnie and Clyde would terrorize the central United States robbing and killing for nearly two years.

Noble knew the Barrows and many other West Dallas toughs. Not unlike them Noble wanted more, much more than the depression and poverty West Dallas offered its indigent residents. Escape for many of them was the outlaw life, which usually meant robbery and running in a fast car. But Noble decided to stay in school, at least until he turned 16, when he bootlegged a bit and signed on to drive a tanker truck for Simms Refinery.

In 1930, Noble married Mildred Bowers, a lovely brunette from West Dallas, and in December of the following year their daughter Freda was born. Noble was arrested for grand theft auto in March 1932, resulting in a two-year suspended sentence. After running afoul of the law, his whereabouts and occupation for the next six years is unclear, although he did tell reporters he had "done some things I'm not proud of."[19]

During Noble's undisclosed travels he gave up truck driving in favor of gambling, and like most young Texans during the Depression likely worked in the East Texas oil fields. Noble had a mechanical aptitude and spent much of his time repairing automobile and airplane engines. It was during this period that he learned to fly and earned a private pilot's license, and more significantly, he met the gambler Sam Murray. The two formed a close working relationship; Noble ran his casino games, provided muscle, and eventually became Murray's personal driver and bodyguard.

By the mid 1930s Murray had seized control of the race wire service for the local area, which gave him virtual control over Dallas bookmaking. Bad blood began to heat up between Binion and Murray in 1938, when, through generous campaign contributions with Dallas city officials, Murray acquired considerable political clout, and began muscling in on the downtown gambling territory controlled by Binion. Despite grave warnings from Binion, Murray continued to edge into Binion's million-dollar-a-year numbers racket. After the warnings, the 54-year-old Murray must have been concerned because he rarely ventured into downtown Dallas, and seldom left the sanctuary of his ranch. When he did, it was always with the protection of his bodyguard, Herbert Noble.

By 1938, the Noble family had moved to Dallas where they rented a small suburban home at 311 Conrad Street. In July, Noble was charged with aggravated assault and carrying a pistol in an incident while carrying out his duties at the Downtown Businessman's Club. Both charges were dismissed.

In public, Noble was always at Murray's side, except to the Dallas National Bank on the morning of June 14, 1940, when Murray was murdered by a lone gunman. With Murray gone, Noble enjoyed a meteoric rise in the Dallas underworld of gambling. Soon after Murray's death he had taken over the games at the Santa Paula Hotel. By the end of World War II, Noble was operating four casinos in downtown Dallas. Binion financed all of Noble's gaming operations, as he had done with Murray, with each location paying a 25 percent tribute. The tribute to Binion covered financing and police protection, which Binion allegedly had in his pocket.

A year after Murray's death, the Nobles purchased 800 acres of ranch land north of Dallas. It featured a large stone-built ranch home with several upscale guest cabins and a nearby airstrip, which rumor had it, Noble used to fly in gamblers to play in a high stakes craps game. Noble also began dealing in used and salvaged aircraft and soon was operating a thriving airplane maintenance business, which served as a front to his lucrative gambling operations. By 1945, Noble was one of Dallas's most potent and best known gamblers, while Mildred lived the life of luxury shopping at Neiman Marcus and driving late-model Cadillacs.

Raymond Laudermilk was another street-wise Dallas gambler who started out parking cars, running errands, and steering for underground gaming parlors. By the early 1920s and 1930s Laudermilk worked for Warren Diamond, protecting games and providing muscle when needed. When Diamond learned he had terminal cancer in 1932, he committed suicide and Laudermilk signed on with his successor, Benny Binion.

Not long after Sam Murray's death in 1940, Murray's widow, Sue, took up with the handsome Laudermilk. Their brief courtship led to marriage during a trip to California, and Raymond and Sue Laudermilk returned to Dallas with a plan. The scheme was the start up of a numbers racket, which had to be authored by Sue, who was bright and ambitious, and had gained experience working the policy game from her late husband, Sam. She figured the racket would be a natural liaison: Sue knew Sam's contacts, how to keep the books, and run the operation; Raymond knew the streets, could oversee the runners, and provide protection and muscle. It seemed that Ray and Sue had everything they needed, except money, and she had a plan for that, too. However, there was one big problem: The Laudermilks would be in direct competition with boss gambler, Benny Binion.

The Laudermilks turned to Sam Murray's ex-bodyguard, Herbert Noble to finance their new endeavor. The ambitious Noble jumped at the proposal. Noble had resented the 25 percent tribute he paid Binion for police protection and the privilege to operate his downtown crap games. He saw the Laudermilks' offer as an opportunity to free himself from Binion's reins, and establish himself as an independent, big-time gambler.

Over the years, Raymond Laudermilk had worked his way up to be the number three man in Binion's numbers racket. He worked the Dallas streets keeping the runners in line, protecting the money, and essentially keeping Benny's policy organization running smoothly. Benny liked Raymond Laudermilk; they were about the same age and had a lot in common—"in their younger years, had worked together with Warren Diamond. Like Binion, Laudermilk was a street gambler who depended for his livelihood on his wits, his nerve, and his ambition."[20]

Binion not only liked Laudermilk, since 1939, he had come to respect his long-time co-worker. That was the year Laudermilk was arrested for felony gambling. The district attorney offered him immunity in exchange for testimony against Benny Binion. When Laudermilk was called to testify, he refused. Laudermilk was fined $500 for contempt of court and he served a brief stint in jail, but the felony gambling charges were dismissed. From then on, Binion became extremely loyal to him.

Had another man attempted to defect and dreamed of being a rival as Laudermilk did, Binion surely wouldn't waste any time taking him out. But Laudermilk was different; the boss gambler valued his loyalty. Binion first offered him a big increase in pay if he stayed in the organization. When Laudermilk declined, Binion offered the raise in pay plus a high-paying job in the organization for Sue. Again, Laudermilk declined. The boss gambler made a final offer: a piece of the action. Knowing that he'd be a marked man, Laudermilk still refused Binion's final offer.

Raymond Laudermilk reasoned that if he lived long enough, he could gather enough money, guns, and influence to shield himself from Binion's revenge. After all, he also had an ace in the hole; Laudermilk knew most of Binion's gunslingers, their faces, and their hangouts, which meant he had a good chance of avoiding them.

THE MURDER OF RAYMOND LAUDERMILK

Almost a year had passed since Raymond Laudermilk had made the crucial decision that he and Sue would be better off defecting from Binion's organization to start up a Dallas numbers racket of their own.

On March 19, 1943, at about nine o'clock at night, several sharp bangs were heard along Ervay Street, near the Ambassador Hotel in downtown Dallas. The unidentified witness called the Dallas Police Department to report what she thought were gun shots and seeing a slender Caucasian man of medium height walking away from a parked car. The man then climbed into the passenger seat of a waiting car, which immediately drove away.

Minutes later, the police arrived to find a lone car parked at the Ambassador's entrance. They found Raymond Laudermilk's lifeless body slouched in the driver's seat with six bullet holes in his chest and stomach.

Within 30 minutes of the shooting, 29-year-old Bob Minyard surrendered to the Dallas County Sheriff's office, announcing that he had just killed Raymond Laudermilk. He confessed that he and Laudermilk "had some trouble" over money, and refused to say any more until he confided with his lawyer.

Minyard's lawyer, Maury Hughes, arrived at the jail about 11p.m. and, after counseling with his new client, spoke on Minyard's behalf. In the words of Hughes, Minyard had just walked out of the Ambassador's lobby, when Laudermilk shouted at him from a parked car. According to Binion's biographer, "He had gone to the passenger side of Laudermilk's car and Laudermilk had angrily demanded that Minyard repay some money he had borrowed. When Minyard replied that he was broke, Laudermilk reached inside his jacket for his pistol, and Minyard fired first in a clear case of self-defense."[21] Hughes also told police that after the shooting, Minyard was able to hitch a ride from a passing car, but realizing he had to surrender, caught a taxi to the sheriff's office. The next day, Minyard was indicted for murder, but he was never tried.

The assassination was effective. Immediately, upon learning of Raymond Laudermilk's murder, Herbert Noble, with no one to oversee his runners, closed his newly established numbers racket. Sue Laudermilk packed her bags and caught the first train leaving Dallas.

Comparable to Hebert Noble's rise after the murder of Sam Murray, Bob Minyard quickly ascended to the top of the Dallas underworld. His career had began humbly with petty thievery and protecting small-time crap games for friends, but soon after the Laudermilk killing, "Minyard acquired, courtesy of Benny Binion, an interest in a prosperous downtown gambling operation."[22] The Dallas kingpin they called "boss gambler," Benny Binion always took care of his friends.

While running his policy racket and underground casino games in Dallas, Benny became involved in a long-running feud with Herbert Noble—a feud that lingered on even after Benny moved to Las Vegas. When Benny suspected Noble, his partner in a downtown craps game, of skimming, he demanded an increase in the cut from 25 to 40 percent of the profits, Noble adamantly refused to comply. Benny then allegedly posted a price on Noble's head of $25,000 and, as a bonus, control of Noble's crap game.

In 1946, Benny lost his political connections and was forced to give up his gambling operations in both Dallas and Fort Worth. He relocated to Las Vegas, where within a year he would found Sin City's most successful casino, and change the style of Western hospitality forever more.

THE SCHEME TO BOMB BINION'S HOME

By the spring of 1950, after miraculously surviving ten assaults on his life, Noble became known around Dallas as "the cat," but unfortunately the 42-year-old target looked the age of a weathered 60-year old. Even worse, at home Noble suffered from the loss of his murdered wife Mildred, as he paced anxiously among the silent rooms that constantly flashed memories of her. Noble hadn't slept much either, as he kept trying to anticipate how and where the next ambush would be orchestrated. To aid his anxiety, Noble acquired six Chihuahuas and turned them loose in the fenced areas around the ranch, figuring that barking dogs would alert him to any possible intruders.

On April 12, Noble was hard at work beneath the wing of his new airplane, a red single-engine Beechcraft he had recently purchased, when the deputy sheriff, George Butler, drove onto the ranch to see him. Since Mildred's murder, Butler usually came out to the ranch every two weeks to update him on the ongoing investigation, and to find out if Noble had picked up any information through his Dallas underworld connections. When Butler approached, the edgy Noble grabbed his rifle and aimed it at him. Butler reacted by stopping in his tracks. Then he inquired, "Herbert, what the hell are you doing? Put that rifle down."

The gambler and the deputy sheriff stood eye to eye until Noble dropped the rifle and sank to his knees sobbing in tears. The boss gambler had murdered his wife, Noble said, and his rival had all the breaks. Binion had all the money, the power and the influence said the stricken gambler. "I never had a chance,"[23] he wept.

Moments later, Noble stood up and regained his composure enough to explain his plan to Butler. Because Noble was in the aircraft salvage trade, he managed to acquire two surplus military bombs, one incendiary and one high explosive. The plan was very basic; Noble intended to terminate his vendetta by bombing Binion's Las Vegas home from a private airplane.

When Butler had approached him, the two three-foot-long bombs lay on the ground in front of the plane where Noble was busy attaching bomb racks to the Beechcraft's wings. Auxiliary fuel tanks had already been fitted in the plane's fuselage, and except for securing the two three-foot-long bombs, Noble's preparations seemed complete. In his pocket Noble carried a detailed map with a target arrow on Binion's home, and surrounding landmarks that could be seen from the air.

Nevertheless, after Butler thought about Noble's bizarre scheme for a moment, he pointed out that even with the auxiliary tanks the plane could never make the flight to Las Vegas. Also Butler said that the return flight might be simple, but no airport in the country would allow a private plane to take off carrying two bombs. Butler finally convinced Noble to rethink his scheme of bombing Binion's home and hand over the map, which in all likelihood, saved the gambler's life.

As Noble grew more cautious trying to avoid another car bombing, he abandoned the Jeep he usually drove to tend the cattle in favor of a small airplane. About once a week Noble would fly over the ranch, and if he spotted anything out of order, send out a ranch hand to make the repair. That's what Noble intended to do on the afternoon of March 22, 1951. But during the darkest hours of early morning, an assailant had wired a nitroglycerine-gel bomb to the generator of Noble's airplane in the same way as Mildred's car. The moment Noble fired the plane's ignition, an explosion blasted off the front of the airplane leaving the engine a gnarled heap. Fortunately, Noble was shielded from the blast by the steel-plated firewall housed between the engine and the cockpit. It allowed him to survive the 11th attempt on his life without any harm.

AUGUST 7, 1951: THE CAT'S LAST LIFE

For more than a week Dallas residents had suffered in the midst of a stifling heat wave. Temperatures had soared to 105° or more, with no clouds in sight to screen the midday sun's oppressive heat.

At eleven thirty on that Tuesday morning, concealed in a thicket of trees on a mound 75 yards east of the Noble's mailbox, two men sat quietly next to a barbed wire fence. Earlier, probably just before dawn, these men had planted a wired wooden box a few inches under the dirt road that ran in front of the mailbox. One of the men held an insulated electrical wire which ran through the grass and weeds to the negative post of a Delco automobile battery hidden in the brush about five yards from the mailbox. Another wire was connected to the positive post of the battery and ran through the grass and weeds to a spot 20 feet from the mailbox and disappeared in the dirt. That wire was attached to a bundle of mercury fulminate detonators nestled in the wooden box that was planted in the road. The box contained a dozen jars of nitroglycerine gel. One hundred yards to the north, shielded from view in a grove of trees, a third man sat behind the wheel of a blue Chevrolet pickup truck with the engine idling.

The mailbox stood at the crux of two county roads that passed through the Noble's 800-acre ranch. From their position atop the mound, the two men in hiding had a clear view of traffic approaching the mailbox from any direction.

At eleven thirty-five a rumble was heard, followed by a moving cloud of dust that signified the approach of a vehicle from the direction of Noble's ranch. The two men watched intently as the automobile, a black 1950 Ford Sedan, pulled up to the mailbox. When they identified the person reaching for his mail was Herb Noble, the man holding the ground wire touched it to the barbed wire fence completing the electrical circuit.

At one fifteen in the afternoon, Gordon Cunningham, who owned the property adjoining Noble's ranch, was the first person to arrive at the scene of what appeared to be a massive explosion. Cunningham drove on to the nearest telephone to alert the sheriff. Within the hour, County Sheriff W.O. Hodges and two Texas Rangers showed up at the scene of the explosion. They saw the mangled chassis of Noble's Ford lying upside down next to a bomb crater four feet deep and six feet across in the road where the mailbox once stood.

Author Gary Sleeper describes the scene of the explosion: "Pieces of Herbert Noble's body were scattered over an area roughly twenty yards in diameter. Ernest Hilliard, a Denton County commissioner who helped gather the remains, described the gruesome task for news reporters. Only Noble's head, shoulders, and arms were intact, he said. The remainder of his body had been blown to shreds. One of his lower legs had been found in the middle of the road about halfway between the bomb crater and the hill where the killers had waited."[24] A photograph of the scene, portrayed on newspaper front pages all over the country showed Noble's demolished car and the bomb crater in the background.

In the eyes of syndicate bosses back East, the nationwide publicity over the Binion/Noble battle was intolerable, drawing unwanted attention to their operations in Dallas and Las Vegas. When Benny's bodyguard, Russian Louis Straus, killed a man in the men's room of the Westerner Club, the syndicate helped the Feds to indict Benny Binion for skimming casino receipts.

Over the years, Binion's Horseshoe became the most profitable casino in Las Vegas. One reason for its success grew from an innovative idea for a tourist attraction: management displayed a large glass-encased horseshoe containing $1 million in $10,000 bills. Tourists loved having their photograph taken in front of the $1 million horseshoe.

CREATION OF THE WORLD SERIES OF POKER

In January 1949, Benny did something that would forever instill the game of poker in the annals of gambling lore. He arranged for Johnny Moss and "Nick the Greek" Dandalos to play heads-up, or head to head, in a poker tournament, which lasted an incredible four months, with Dandalos losing a reported $400,000.

Over the years Benny continued establishing heads-up contests between high-stakes players. In 1970 the seed of an idea began to germinate and he invited six of the best-known poker players to compete in a tournament for cash. After a set time the participants voted, by secret ballot, to determine the winner.

Benny's creation of the WSOP encouraged the popularity of poker, and with the help of wide spread television coverage, poker's popularity blossomed and grew. Several memorable moments have occurred during the WSOP's Main Event. One well-known moment was Jack Straus's miraculous comeback win in 1982. He pushed his chips forward and lost. But getting up from the table, he discovered one $500 chip under a napkin, and from that single chip, Straus ultimately won the tournament. The incident eventually became known as "A chip and a chair," which means that's all a player truly needs to win a tournament—one chip and a seat in the event.

Another memorable moment occurred when Chris Moneymaker won the event in 2003, earning over $2 million. All he'd invested was $40 to play in an online qualifying event. This amazing feat, labeled "The Moneymaker Effect," inspired millions of would-be poker players worldwide to try their luck. In 2006, the main event by itself peaked at 8,773 participants, with the eventual champion, Jamie Gold, winning a record prize of $12 million!

Though he never held a gaming license after 1953, Benny Binion still was a respected casino entrepreneur, a living legend of Sin City's shadowy past. Author Gary Sleeper wrote, "Young Vegas entrepreneurs like Steve Wynn came to him for advice. The University of Nevada studied his marketing techniques in its School of Casino Management."[25] With his son Jack, Benny was able to relocate the National Finals Rodeo to Las Vegas in 1985, where it has since remained. Benny never forgot his Texas roots, nor did he overlook the cowboys whenever they came to town. He always paid their entry fees for the championship event.

Benny loved talking about the old days and even agreed to record a lengthy oral interview with the History Department of the University of Nevada. As you would expect, the subject of Herb Noble would come up, and author Gary Sleeper described the following scenario: "As always, Benny denied any involvement with Noble's murder, but he couldn't resist a hint. The twinkle in his eye must have been blinding when he said:"

> *Well, you know them things. There's a little stuff in the Green Felt Jungle that they got from the records. And there's a damn lot that ain't, you know. Anywhere there's smoke, is a little bit of fire. I've done nothin' to nobody that I didn't think it was goin' to do me some bodily harm. There's no way in the world I'd harm anybody for any amount of money. But if anybody goes to talkin' about doin' me bodily harm, or my family bodily harm, I'm very capable, thank God, for really takin' care of 'em in a most artistic way.*[26]

DEATH OF A LEGEND

In the Spring of 1989, Benny Binion sat down for an in-depth interview with a reporter from the *Houston Chronicle*. Benny summarized his Dallas bootlegging days in a nutshell: "Used to really live dangerous in them days. And I *was* dangerous. I wouldn't do to be screwed around with. I used to get a kick out of it. But I don't do that no more."[27]

After Benny lost his Nevada gaming license, he spent a lot of his time trading horses to rodeo contractors from his 250,000 acre ranch situated in the "Big Open" country along the Yellowstone River near Jordan, Montana.

About six months after the interview on Christmas Day, 1989 Benny passed away. The much loved and colorful gambler's gambler died of a heart attack at the age of 85. A year later, Benny was posthumously inducted into the Poker Hall of Fame. His old friend "Amarillo Slim" Preston, another poker legend, suggested this epitaph: "He was either the gentlest bad guy or the baddest good guy you'd ever seen."[28]

* * *

Chapter 2

THE KEFAUVER HEARINGS

UNEARTHS THE MOB

"*The Mafia is a shadowy international organization that lurks behind much of*

America's organized criminal activity. It is an organization about which none of its members, on fear of death, will talk. In fact, some of its witnesses called before us, who we had good reason to believe could tell us about the Mafia, sought to dismiss it as a sort of fairy tale, or legend that children hear in Sicily, where the Mafia originated. The Mafia, however, is no fairy tale. It is ominously real, and it has scarred the face of America with almost every conceivable type of criminal violence, including murder, traffic in narcotics, smuggling, extortion, white slavery, kidnapping, and labor racketeering." [29]

— Senator Estes Kefauver speaking as
chairman in 1950 at the Special Committee to
Investigate Crime in Interstate Commerce

In 1950, for the first time, Americans focused on the Mafia and organized crime. Estes Kefauver, the Democratic Senator from Tennessee, chaired televised hearings of the Special Committee to Investigate Crime in Interstate Commerce, popularly known as the Kefauver Committee. The first committee of its kind, it was composed of senators from around the country ordered to expose organized crime in America for the evil empire that it was. A second purpose was to gain a better understanding of how to fight it. The public's sentiment was reflected in a *Life* magazine article of April 6, 1951: "People had suddenly gone indoors into living rooms, taverns, and clubrooms, auditoriums and back-offices. There, in eerie half-light, looking at millions of small frosty screens, people sat as if charmed. Never before had the attention of the nation been riveted so completely on a single matter."[30]

The hearings became the surprise television hit of the year as all three major networks interrupted their regularly scheduled programming to air the proceedings live. "Household chores, office work, and factory schedules were put aside as people became glued to the TV. The New York sessions were the climax to nine months of hearings in 14 cities. During the course of the investigation, witnesses were murdered and public officials were disgraced. Most important, shadowy underworld figures were made highly visible," [31] wrote author Thomas Reppetto.

The hearings included testimony from the likes of Frank Costello, Tony Accardo, Meyer Lansky, Mickey Cohen, and Willie Moretti, as they all took the Fifth Amendment, unwilling to incriminate themselves over their shady business dealings. To a

41

man they denied ties to the Mafia, La Cosa Nostra, the Chicago Outfit, or the East Coast Mob—which the committee labeled organized crime. Under oath, some claimed never to have heard of the Mafia. Others ventured to say that they may have read about the Mafia once or twice in newspapers.

Back in the early days of legalized gaming in Nevada, before the Gaming Control Board was established in 1955, licensees were approved despite numerous minor gambling violations, even if they had a history of violence. The Tax Commission kept these behaviors on file, yet with few exceptions the only real background analysis the Commission received came from a satellite office of the FBI.

When visitors from back east came to Las Vegas they often wisecracked about the presence of so many wise guys on the casino floor. Visitors remembered them from the illegal gambling joints back home—Cleveland, Steubenville, Boston, Miami, Chicago, and New York. Nevertheless, the remote desert oasis of Las Vegas seemed immune to exposure as a town run by men who fronted for the hoodlum element. That was until the infamous Apalachin Mafia conference was uncovered November 14, 1957, at the home of mobster Joseph "Joe the Barber" Barbara in up-state New York. Peter Maas in *The Valachi Papers*, has written, "It was attended by roughly 100 Mafiosi from the United States, Canada, and Italy. Expensive cars with license plates from around the country aroused the curiosity of local and state law enforcement that raided the meeting, causing Mafiosi to flee into the woods and the area surrounding the Barbara estate. More than 60 underworld bosses were detained and indicted." [32]

Discovery of the Apalachin Mafia meeting helped confirm

the existence of organized crime in America, which some, including FBI Director J. Edgar Hoover, had long refused to acknowledge. It also initiated greater police investigation about the presence of organized crime in American society. Even before New York's Mafia conference was exposed, starting in 1950 with the Kefauver Hearings, Nevada legislators wanted to avoid federal intervention into Mob activities.

Kefauver's focus on organized crime, which led to an overall increase in federal law-enforcement interest in Mob activity, foretold a special awareness on the high-profile Las Vegas. That focus, coupled with the ongoing threat of federal taxation of the state's gaming revenue, produced a significant countermeasure by Nevada legislators: creation of a two-tiered entity of casino regulation in the form of the Gaming Control Board and the Gaming Commission. The Gaming Control Board had the investigative function, gathering information and weighing the data it collected. They then made recommendations to the Gaming Commission, which had the final say. The new regulatory structure had two positive effects on Nevada. It kept the Feds from getting involved, and it gave Nevada some degree of credibility for controlling its top industry, lacking ever since gaming was legalized in 1931.

THE MOB COMES TO LAS VEGAS

Why did this "shadowy international organization" want to come to Las Vegas? The allure of Vegas is embedded in its past when two significant events happened to coincide many years ago. Between 1919 and 1933, America was in the midst of National Prohibition, which, in simple terms, made it unlawful to manufacture and distribute alcohol. Combined with the Great Depression, which began in October 1929 and lasted 11 years, the "Noble Experiment" called Prohibition provided a great opportunity to bootleggers who supplied illegal moonshine to a thirsty America. During this era the average worker earned $2,000 annually, but the average bootlegger earned that much in two weeks. And big-time bootleggers, such as Al Capone and Tony Cornero—the first gangster to build a casino away from downtown Las Vegas—made untold millions. In the midst of all this, in 1931 gambling is legalized in Nevada.

By 1931 Prohibition had endured 12 years, and everyone knew it was a huge failure. In the first year alone more than 1,000 people died consuming poisonous moonshine—three times that number died the following year—and the bootleggers became rich. Many producers of illegal rot-gut alcohol simply didn't care whether or not their brew killed people, they were greedy and in it for the money. One nameless bootlegger once said in an interview, "America is going to have its liquor, one way or another."[33]

With the handwriting on the wall, the bootleggers had come to realize that it was just a matter of time before Prohibition would be repealed, and they'd be out of business. With time running out, it seemed only natural for these rumrunners, flush with an abundance of cash, to invest their ill-gotten gains in the only state in America where gambling was legal.

Las Vegas, though, was not their original choice. When mobsters first came to Nevada they were drawn to Reno. They could see it was a thriving city, a good place to do business. But their applications to build or buy out existing casinos were turned down. The city fathers wanted nothing to do with gangsters. Unable to get a toehold there, they came south to Las Vegas.

Mobsters of every stripe came to Las Vegas: ex-bootleggers, hoods, thieves, loan sharks, and killers—Sin City's founding fathers. Their influence lasted almost 50 years, and their impact on those formative years will forever be ingrained in the lore of the city. During its heyday The Mob controlled almost every sizable casino resort along the Fabulous Las Vegas Strip, stealing untold millions in cash from casino count rooms.

Before such legends as Benjamin "Bugsy Siegel" and ex-Dallas Mob boss Benny Binion came to Vegas, an enterprising Italian immigrant with a sordid past named Tony Cornero arrived in 1931. Like many other men in Prohibition era America, Cornero made big money as a bootlegger furnishing thirsty southern California drinkers with illegal spirits. When gaming was legalized in Nevada, Cornero, along with his two brothers relocated to Las Vegas and built the first casino resort situated away from downtown. Years later, Cornero would found the infamous Stardust Casino, the source of Martin Scorcesse's famous film *Casino*.

Others mobsters are scarcely remembered, such as the two who dared to rob the Flamingo in 1951, Tony Trombino and Tony Brancato—known as the "Dumb Tonys," so-named for foolishly robbing a Mob-run casino. Within a year, both were assassinated.

The crime remained unsolved until 1977 when Hollywood gangster Jimmy "The Weasel" Fratiano turned state's evidence and admitted to the killing.

After the double assassinations, no one robbed the Flamingo again. The Mob, just like legitimate business men, knew the value of advertising. Other memorable Vegas mobsters with provocative nicknames included two of the city's most notorious: Benjamin "Bugsy" Siegel and Tony "the Ant" Spilotro. Neither man liked his moniker. Siegel earned his early growing up in New York City. When angered or thwarted he was said to "go buggy." He preferred to be called Ben. Spilotro's nickname was adopted by the media after FBI agent William F. Roemer Jr. referred to him as "a little pissant." Unable to publish the term, the media simply used the expression "Ant."

When Prohibition ended in 1933, the bootleggers were virtually out of the booze business, and The Mob found itself looking for new sources of revenue. Casinos seemed a natural attraction, and Nevada's recent legalization of gaming offered a tremendous opportunity for legitimate profit.

Soon after gambling was legalized in Nevada in 1931, other racket bosses and bootleggers like Tony Cornero flocked into the state seeking refuge from the law. Historian Alan Balboni wrote, "Providing liquor and gambling to Americans in the 1920s and 1930s was a somewhat dangerous enterprise, yet one that provided opportunities for wealth and power for those willing to take the risk. Rare indeed was a Las Vegas Strip founding father in the two decades after World War II who had not been involved in manufacturing or distributing liquor in the 1920s."[34]

A WIDE-OPEN CITY

Before the Gaming Control Board was created, acquiring a gaming license in Las Vegas was a simple process. Gaming had been under the jurisdiction of the county sheriff's department and the Nevada Tax Commission. In fact, prior to 1955 new buyers of an existing casino could be "grandfathered" into being approved for ownership, which meant they would not have to apply for a new license. Instead, new owners could take over the existing gaming license with no questions asked.

From 1931 to the mid-1960s Las Vegas was a wide-open city—open to mobsters, to gamblers, to hookers, and to money launderers. Vegas was wide-open in another sense—it was free of regulation. The absence of cameras on either casino floors or counting rooms facilitated skimming, the practice of withdrawing a share of the income for management and for investors—who were mostly Mob bosses—and thereby lower the gross income reported to the IRS. The absence of limits on cash transactions and minimal reporting requirements made Vegas a haven for money laundering. Casinos were virtual forests where, as Meyer Lansky once observed, "You simply shook the trees and watched thousand dollar bills fall like leaves."[35]

So without stringent control, beginning in 1931, when gambling became legal in Nevada, the resort casinos began sprouting up like tulips in spring. The first carpet joint away from downtown was Tony Cornero's Green Meadows. Later, the El Rancho Vegas in 1941 became the first located along what was to become the hallowed Las Vegas Strip. Then in 1943 came the Last Frontier, and downtown arose the Nevada Biltmore, and El

Cortez. Three years later, the Golden Nugget, and more noteworthy Ben Siegel's Flamingo opened in December of 1946.

The surge of carpet joints continued when the Thunderbird opened on the Strip in 1947, and the Desert Inn began operations in 1950. Two years later in 1952, the Sahara opened, with each of the following resorts opening in consecutive years; the Sands, the Riviera, the Dunes, the Hacienda, the Tropicana and the Mint downtown, and the Stardust in 1958. The Castaways opened its doors in 1963, and three years later, Caesars Palace, the Aladdin and the Four Queens opened theirs. In 1967 the Frontier Hotel emerged, with Circus-Circus, the Landmark, and the Las Vegas Hilton opening in consecutive years.

Today there are the huge themed resorts: including Aria, Paris, Mirage, Treasure Island, Palms, the Rio, Ballys, Sam's Town, Excalibur, New York New York, the Bellagio, Mandalay Bay, Luxor, the MGM Grand, Cosmopolitan, and the Venetian. There's also the non-themed Wynn and Encore, along with the huge CityCenter project, not to mention plans for numerous other multi-billion dollar mega resorts with luxurious condominiums.

* * *

Chapter 3

TONY CORNERO—THE "ADMIRAL" WHO FOUNDED THE STARDUST

*a*gainst the backdrop of Prohibition and the Great Depression, the gangster Tony Cornero's storied life of running gambling ships and operating Las Vegas casinos was as vibrant as a modern-day soap opera. Anthony "Tony" Cornero made his name and most of his money during the mid 1930s and 1940s, bootlegging and running two illegal gambling ships off the coast of Southern California. His alias was Tony Stralla, with nicknames "Tony the Hat," and the "Admiral."

Cornero's varied criminal career began soon after he and his family immigrated to America from northern Italy. At age 16 he was arrested for robbery and sentenced to 10 months in reform school. During the next ten years he established a lengthy criminal record, including three counts of attempted murder and two counts of bootlegging. In the early 1920s, when Cornero was not incarcerated, he made a living driving a taxi in San Francisco.

In 1923, with Prohibition the law of the land, Cornero became a rumrunner, supplying much of southern California's underground nightclubs and high-class clientele with illicit booze. Like today's drug runners who traffic contraband onto Florida beaches using high speed "cigar boats," Cornero smuggled Canadian whiskey, and Mexican and Caribbean rum, onto Southern California beaches using shrimp boats capable of outrunning the U.S. Coast Guard's antiquated and undermanned vessels. Cornero's skills as a bootlegger made him a millionaire by the age of 25.

One fateful night in 1926, authorities caught up with Cornero returning from Mexico with an estimated 1,000 cases of rum. He was arrested and sentenced to two years' imprisonment, but while in transit to prison by rail, Cornero escaped and jumped off the train. From there the fugitive managed to elude his captors and eventually boarded a ship for Vancouver, British Columbia. When he reached Europe, Cornero remained in hiding until 1929, when he returned to Los Angeles and turned himself in to authorities. Cornero served his two years in prison, and soon after his release in 1931 he reestablished himself in Culver City, California, as a big-time bootlegger producing up to 5,000 gallons of booze daily. With the repeal of Prohibition in 1933, Cornero and his two brothers, Louis and Frank, moved to Las Vegas intending to establish a legitimate casino.

CORNERO'S GREEN MEADOWS VENTURE

After moving to Las Vegas, Tony Cornero and his brothers purchased a 30-acre site along Fremont Street near the intersection of East Charleston, a location farther east than the established sawdust joints downtown. There, the Corneros created the upscale Green Meadows. Compared to the existing downtown casinos such as the El Cortez and Apache Hotel, the Meadows was considered a most impressive facility. Virtually all of the downtown so-called "pedestrian" joints attracted people dressed in jeans and boots. However, photographs taken at the Meadows' grand opening show many guests from Las Vegas' professional and business elite dressed in suits and evening attire. Although the hotel had only 30 sleeping rooms, they were "all with bath," as the local newspaper pointed out, with hot water available at all hours. The hotel's public relations person planted the news article to emphasize that the Meadows had electric lights. Jack Laughlin, producer of such well-known stage shows as "No, No, Nanette" was hired to create the "Meadows Revue." Another draw at the Meadows was the Cornero brothers' bootlegged Canadian whiskey, unavailable to patrons of competing casinos, who managed to imbibe the inferior "bathtub" booze made in nearby North Las Vegas and Lincoln County.

When the Meadows began making big money, Tony Cornero started investing in other local casinos. His newfound success soon lured unwanted attention from the wrong people. East Coast syndicate leaders Charlie Luciano and Meyer Lansky tried to muscle in on the Meadows' gaming profits. Cornero's refusal to comply led to the breakout of a gang war. It ended rather quickly when his enemies torched and burned the Meadows to the ground in May 1932, and Cornero simply gave up. Disappointed, the former rumrunner-turned-casino-entrepreneur sold his Las Vegas interests and moved back to Los Angeles.

CASINOS AFLOAT

In 1938 Tony Cornero decided to operate shipboard gambling in international waters, where he figured to avoid interference from the law. He purchased two large ships and transformed them into luxurious floating casinos. His premiere cruise ship, the SS Rex, could accommodate 2,000 gamblers in addition to 350 crew including gourmet chefs. Its first-class dining room offered French cuisine exclusively, a complete orchestra, tuxedo-clad croupiers, waiters, waitresses, and armed security guards. Most patrons who came aboard were wealthy southern Californians from Long Beach and Santa Monica. They arrived via 25-cent water taxies beyond the "three mile limit," where the gambling ships were anchored. Both of Cornero's floating casinos reportedly earned a staggering profit of $300,000 a night.

Cornero's nefarious prosperity set off outrage and condemnation from California authorities. The newly appointed district attorney, Earl Warren, ordered a series of raids intended to shut down gambling ships outside California waters. For nearly eight years Cornero battled with state authorities over their jurisdiction and the legality of their entering international waters. One such raid occurred in May 1946, after Earl Warren became governor of California. Authorities refigured the starting point of the three-mile limit, thereby bringing the gambling ships under California jurisdiction. Police boarded several Coast Guard cutters and motored out to the gambling ships to shut them down and arrest Cornero. When the cutters arrived, Cornero had a surprise for the police who tried to board. He ordered the ship's fire hoses turned on them, reportedly yelling at the boarders that they were committing piracy on the high seas. The confrontation lasted three days before Cornero surrendered. The Coast Guard confiscated the SS Rex, and soon after, Cornero closed down his other gambling ship, the SS Tango.

In his next venture Tony Cornero tried to establish illegal land-based casinos in Los Angeles, but was thwarted by the West Coast Mob's emissary, Mickey Cohen, who warned Cornero to stay out of his territory. Taking the notorious gangster's warning seriously, Cornero returned to Las Vegas.

ATTEMPTED MURDER AND STARDUST MEMORIES

In Las Vegas, Cornero made a deal to lease the Apache Hotel and name it the Rex. At first the Las Vegas City Council voted in favor of Cornero's gaming license despite knowing of his criminal background, his history with the Meadows, and his gambling ships off the California coast. Several months later the Council reconsidered the issue and revoked his gaming license, closing the Rex.

Again, Tony Cornero moved back to Los Angeles and began making plans to build a casino south of San Diego, in Mexico's Baja California. On February 9, 1948, after returning from Mexico, an event happened he never could have anticipated. Two Mexicans appeared mysteriously at Cornero's home in Beverly Hills. One held a carton, the other knocked on the door. When Cornero opened the door, the man holding the carton said, "Here, Cornero, this is for you," pulled out a handgun, and shot him four times in the stomach. "It was a clear message from the casino owners of Las Vegas. Expertise about running casinos should not be shared with our neighbors to the South, who had the intention of taking business away from Las Vegas,"[36] wrote Steve Fischer in *When The Mob Ran Vegas*.

Critically wounded, Cornero underwent surgery that night and survived, returning once again to Las Vegas. The year was 1955. He decided to build another hotel casino much larger than the Green Meadows, on the old Los Angeles Highway (State

Highway 91), nicknamed "the Strip." He purchased a 40-acre site on the west side just south of Sahara Avenue and considered calling the project the Starlite Hotel and Casino.

To raise money to build the plushest hotel on the old Los Angeles Highway, Cornero began selling shares of stock in his Starlite project. Like most underworld men of the time, he didn't worry about the finer points of federal or state law. Nor was he prudent with his bookkeeping. He was known to keep records of investments in his head or on matchbook covers he carried in his pocket. Conceivably, $20,000 would earn the investor four percent of net profits from the keno parlor, or three percent of the profits from the showroom. Even though Cornero kept careless records, over the years he developed a reputation as a very productive earner.

Meanwhile, construction began on the Starlite. Not until later that year after the casino complex was half built, did Cornero make application to the Nevada Gaming Commission for a gaming license. They turned him down. Not to be denied, Cornero approached his friend Milton B. "Farmer" Page and inquired if he would "front" for the Starlite. Page accepted, on condition that he would be in charge of running it. While all this was taking place, construction of the casino complex progressed, the price of building materials soared, and Cornero ran out of construction funds.

Cornero envisioned Las Vegas much as it would become in later years, with spacious casinos replacing the sawdust-floored dives that sported two or three tables. Toward that end, he planned the Starlite as more than a casino—he planned a grand resort to attract the wealthy clientele who once frequented his offshore gambling ships. Mirroring his strategy of providing convenient boat transportation from the shores of California to his floating casinos, Cornero built a landing strip in Vegas for small aircraft to ferry wealthy gamblers to his resort.

Rather than halt construction on the Starlite when he ran out of money, Cornero approached Moe Dalitz and his partner in New York, Meyer Lansky. Offering the Stardust as collateral, Cornero obtained $1.25 million in the first of at least three loans. As the Starlite neared completion, he called a meeting of his investors for July 31, 1955, to explain the need for another infusion of $800,000 to stock the resort with food, liquor, and enough cash on-hand for all the casino cages.

SUSPICIOUS END FOR THE ADMIRAL

Alas, Tony Cornero died July 31, 1955, the same day of his investors' meeting, never to see the Starlite completed. He spent his final moments shooting dice on the casino floor of Moe Dalitz's Desert Inn. According to witnesses, all of a sudden Cornero grabbed his stomach and dropped dead. Although no autopsy was performed, the official coroner's report determined that he died of natural causes. Nevertheless, rumors flew that his drink had been poisoned. Mysteriously, his body was removed from the casino floor before the Sheriff's Department or the coroner was contacted. Something else was suspicious too—the glass Cornero had been drinking from was conveniently removed and washed. The police never had the opportunity to examine it.

The day after Cornero's demise, Las Vegas newspapers

carried front-page stories about his life and death. *Review-Journal* reporter Bob Holdorf best captured the circumstances of his death:

> Tony died the way he had lived.
>
> He died at a gambling table.
>
> Probably, the diminutive gambler was happy as hell when he felt the surging heat whip across his chest, and blot out the world.
>
> What other way was there for him to go?
>
> In a bed? Never!
>
> In a gun battle? They tried that!
>
> In an ambush? They tried that, too!
>
> Tony went the way any tough gambling hombre wants to get it. Fast and painless! The pain that hit Tony Cornero
>
> Stralla lasted something less than 10 seconds and then it was all over.
>
> He had crapped out.[37]

After Cornero's passing, Moe Dalitz and his Mob pals supervised the completion of a slightly less luxurious Stardust than Cornero had pictured. Eventually new management renamed it the Stardust Resort and Casino, and when it opened in 1958, it was the largest hotel in the world, eventually becoming a colossal success that endured 48 years.

During its colorful, history the "mobbed up" Stardust was a major source of intrigue for the film *Casino*. In the 1970s, the FBI exposed the Stardust's owner, "Argent Corporation," in the largest skimming operation ever reported. Between $7 and $15 million had been siphoned off using rigged scales to underestimate weighed coins taken from slot machines. The FBI's investigation into the Stardust's skimming operations resulted, in 1984, in the highest fine ever issued by Nevada's Gaming Commission, $3 million. The Chicago Outfit sold the resort the following year to a locally owned, respected, legitimate gaming company, the Boyd Group. The Boyd family was surprised when an accurate accounting of the casino's receipts showed enormous profits.

In *The Enforcer*, one of several books written by an ex-FBI senior agent in the Bureau's Chicago organized-crime squad, author William F. Roemer Jr. wrote: "The amount of skim had been so heavy, that the profit and loss statement did not present a true picture of the gold mine the Stardust was."[38] When Boyd Gaming closed the doors on this infamous resort in November 2006, anticipating to replace it with a more modern complex of resort hotels and convention facilities, the final chapter of this storied resort casino was written.

* * *

Chapter 4

BENJAMIN "BUGSY" SIEGEL

Nowadays when people think of Las Vegas, they tend to associate it with the legendary mobster Benjamin "Bugsy" Siegel and his affiliation with the Flamingo Hotel & Casino. Many of the same people, especially those who have seen the 1991 film *Bugsy* starring Warren Beatty, are under the impression that the Flamingo was Bugsy Siegel's concept. From there, it is easy to see how an eccentric killer could be endowed in legend as the creator of the modern city of Las Vegas. The film's closing

60

credits give further credence to this deeply rooted legend by claiming the events portrayed were based in fact.

Truth be known, Bugsy—with financial assistance from Meyer Lansky's East Coast Syndicate—took over the famed Flamingo resort from its creator long after construction began. In reality, it was the Flamingo's founder who purchased the 33-acre site, conceptualized the original architectural plans, completed one third of the project's construction, and depleted all of his construction funding before Bugsy and the boys got involved.

If not Bugsy Siegel, then who was the true founder of the famed Flamingo? This is the mega casino-hotel that evolved into the fabulous Las Vegas Strip, the gaming and entertainment capital of the world! Contrary to the fictionalized film version, the creator of the Flamingo was a successful nightclub owner and acclaimed publisher of the *Hollywood Reporter*. His name was William R. "Billy" Wilkerson, and he earned his notoriety and much of his wealth from the five nightclubs he built along Hollywood's glamorous Sunset Strip during the 1930s and early 1940s.

Wilkerson's experience as a shrewd nightclub owner together with his love of gambling inevitably led him to Las Vegas, where he bought the 33-acre site on which the Flamingo stands today. Through his architect George Russell, Wilkerson designed and built the initial stages of the famed resort before Bugsy and The Mob bailed out the troubled publisher with an influx of $1 million cash, incorporated with an offer he couldn't refuse.

Under Bugsy's rein, the Flamingo turned out to be a huge

flop, and by June of 1946, through massive cost overruns and embezzlement of construction funds, it all came to a bloody end for the flamboyant mobster. But after his demise, by the spring of 1947, under control of the Flamingo's new general manager Gus Greenbaum, the resort-casino became very profitable earning more that $2 million as Sin City's first mega resort.

No one personified The Mob in Las Vegas more than Benjamin Siegel, the psychotic hoodlum given the moniker "Bugsy." A reputably successful gangster, Siegel however, turned out to be a terrible builder and businessman. In Vegas lore he will forever be remembered by his connections to the renowned Flamingo and his outrageous girlfriend Virginia Hill.

As time marches on, continued persistence of the myth that the Flamingo was Ben Siegel's idea tells you something about how legends are made. Over the years Siegel was erroneously credited for everything from putting the glamour into today's fabulous Strip resorts to inventing Las Vegas itself. Nevertheless, few appreciate just how big a gangster he truly was.

EARLY YEARS

No one knows exactly where and when Ben Siegel began killing. Given his sociopathic behavior, many experts believe he may have started his murderous ways in his early teens. Born Benjamin Siegelbaum in Brooklyn, New York, in 1905, he began his life of crime as a young boy. At first it was simple theft; then he and an accomplice, a young Moe Sedway graduated to shaking down pushcart merchants on Manhattan's lower east side. After shortening his name to Siegel, he devised a protection racket whereby vulnerable street peddlers were forced to pay a dollar a day to avoid their merchandise being incinerated.

While still a teenager, Siegel joined up with Meyer Lansky— a friendship that evolved into the notorious syndicate Murder Incorporated. Early on, the two men were known for their viciousness even while their operation concentrated primarily on car theft, gambling, and extortion. Eventually they graduated to a string of killings on behalf of the New York bootlegging community to which they now belonged. At the age of 23, Siegel married his high school sweetheart, Esta, the sister of another Mob hit man, Whitey Krakower. Siegel and Esta had two daughters, though the marriage ended in divorce as a result of Siegel's notorious womanizing.

Through Lansky, Siegel met and became friends with Charles "Lucky" Luciano who later established the National Syndicate the governing body of the country's five organized crime families. A year later, Siegel and Lansky began building ties to Frank Costello, future bosses of the Genovese crime family. In 1931 Siegel, Albert Anastasia, Joe Adonis, and Vito Genovese formed the team that assassinated Mob boss Joe Masseria paving the way for Luciano's rise to the top of the Syndicate. By then, Siegel and Lansky were firmly planted in the booze smuggling business.

Ten years later, following the repeal of National Prohibition Siegel and Lansky switched from bootlegging to racketeering, including gambling, bookmaking, and running numbers. Siegel established himself in a suite at the Waldorf Astoria, where he lived in high style surrounded by bodyguards. He also traveled in a bullet-proof limousine.

SIEGEL ACQUITTED IN GREENBERG MURDER TRIAL

In November 1939, Siegel was tried for the murder of Harry Greenberg who had become a police informant. He was eventually acquitted of the charge when the only witness mysteriously disappeared, but all the publicity surrounding Siegel's trial affected his reputation. He especially hated the nickname "Bugsy," which the press popularized during the trial. The name, a synonym for crazy, originated from his youth on the streets of Brooklyn, where he was known for his crazy rages and psychopathic behavior. No one who valued his life used the nickname to Siegel's face.

Stories of Siegel's violence and intimidation were commonplace in Las Vegas. Once a tourist failed to refer to the boss by his proper name and instead addressed him as Bugsy. Siegel beat the tourist bloody with his ever-present .38 revolver. In another incident, Siegel forced hotel publicist Abe Schiller to crawl on his hands and knees around the Flamingo's pool after Schiller referred to the gangster's past and raised a question about the Bugsy nickname.

Despite alleged involvement in crimes of bootlegging, prostitution, loan sharking, drug trafficking, and murder, Ben Siegel managed to avoid being convicted of any serious charges. He also had the looks of a leading man of Hollywood. ·

SIEGEL'S FASCINATION WITH HOLLYWOOD

A number of published sources list Ben Siegel as one of the most feared and respected members of the East Coast Syndicate. Siegel not only evolved into a big-time earner for his syndicate pals, but he also became a very wealthy man in his own right. Some say that while out west he wanted to become an actor. In any case he became captivated with Hollywood and loved to hobnob with Hollywood stars, including Jean Harlow and George Raft. In Hollywood, Siegel led two lives; he was seducing starlets and running with the Hollywood crowd, but at the same time, he was expanding his underworld activities, which included extorting money from gangster Tony Cornero's offshore gambling enterprises, muscling in on the businesses of nearby racetracks, investing in prostitution rings, and trafficking in illegal drugs from Mexico. Hardly an illegal activity existed in the American Southwest that didn't involve Ben Siegel.

THE MOB'S WIRE SERVICE FOR BOOKIES

Siegel took an interest in Las Vegas and began buying into small casinos, while his friend Lansky concentrated on the El Cortez. His biggest moneymaker, however, was the wire service a revenue stream that reportedly produced $25,000 a month.

During the early 1940s the East Coast Mob sent Ben Siegel west to oversee and expand their national race and wire service for bookies. This wire service was crucial to Las Vegas bookmakers: without it, they could be driven into bankruptcy by past-posting bettors—betting after races were decided. The Mob knew that if they could control the wire service, they could also control the bookies.

According to author Steve Fischer, "Ben Siegel came to Las Vegas in 1941, the same time that the Nevada legislature voted to legalize horseracing results by wire. Ben invested his own money, and lots of his partners' money, in a variety of early Las Vegas ventures. He bought points in the Las Vegas Club and the Boulder Club and Golden Nugget downtown, sold for a profit, and decided he wanted to try his luck out on the Strip, what was then called Highway 91. So he bought a piece of the Last Frontier from Bill Moore the manager and co-owner."[39] Fischer also notes that, "Ben had a very persuasive argument. Each of these properties needed the income that came from bets on horseracing. In the 1940s and early 1950s, horse parlors didn't belong to the hotels, they were leased space. The owners of the horse parlors paid rent to the hotel and also paid a percentage of the profit. Ben Siegel owned the Trans America Wire Service, which was a monopoly. So, if one of the resorts out on the Strip, or one of the casinos downtown wanted to add a horse parlor to its income, it also added Ben Siegel as a partner. And in adding Ben Siegel, they were adding Ben's partners, Meyer Lansky and Frank Costello.[40]

It was during this period out west that Siegel likely became acquainted with Billy Wilkerson at Ciro's nightclub in Beverly Hills, which was one of five popular upscale nightclubs owned by Wilkerson. Siegel also recruited Los Angeles gang boss Mickey Cohen as his lieutenant and moved Esta and their two daughters,

Barbara and Millicent, to California. FBI reports noted that Siegel claimed on his tax return to earn his living through legal gambling at the Santa Anita race track.

Besides Ben Siegel's allure with Hollywood, people close to him knew that he craved legitimacy and respectability. Those qualities, however, always seemed beyond his reach. Years later, everything would change when The Mob placed Siegel in charge of overseeing their interest in a new air-cooled hotel being built in Las Vegas, giving him a second opportunity to reinvent himself.

* * *

Chapter 5

BILLY WILKERSON'S FLAMINGO

"After my father's death in 1962, I began hearing family stories about his pivotal role in Las Vegas history. For this reason, I eagerly anticipated the Warren Beatty film "Bugsy" which was released in December 1991. Sadly, the story on-screen bore little relationship to my treasured family memories." [41]

—From W.R. Wilkerson III, author of the book *The Man Who Invented Las Vegas*

EARLY LIFE

*B*orn in September 1890 in Nashville, *Tennessee, Billy Wilkerson developed an early interest in the medical field.* After his family relocated to Philadelphia, Pennsylvania, he began studying medicine until his father, a renowned gambler, died unexpectedly and left behind a

huge mountain of debt. Wilkerson was forced to give up his medical training and find employment to support himself and his mother.

A short time later, in a stroke of luck for Wilkerson, a friend from medical school placed a World Series wager and won. "The prize" was a small Nickelodeon in Fort Lee, New Jersey, which Wilkerson agreed to manage in exchange for a share of the profits. Visions of a medical career faded into memory as Wilkerson discovered his penchant for the fledgling movie industry. Between 1918 and 1929, he held a variety of movie-related jobs from the production of one-reelers to sales. During this period he also served as District Manager for Universal Pictures, which led him to abandon the East Coast for Southern California, the heart of the movie industry. There, he turned his earlier investment in a New York trade paper into the first daily trade paper for the motion picture industry.

WILKERSON MOVES TO HOLLYWOOD

In October 1929, at the age of 39, Billy Wilkerson intended to leave New York City and begin a new life in California. To do so, he sold his interest in his daily trade paper for $20,000. Unfortunately, he met a stockbroker, took his advice, and invested the entire proceeds, plus a $25,000 loan, in the stock market. That ill-fated day was Black Tuesday the day the stock market crashed and set off The Great Depression. Almost penniless, and in debt as his father had been, Wilkerson left New York City the same afternoon, and with his wife and daughter, motored cross-country to make their home in Hollywood.

Less than a year later and with the help of investors who believed in his trade paper idea, Wilkerson realized his dream with publication of his first edition of the *Hollywood Reporter*. The magazine "reported on movies, studios, and personalities in an outrageously candid style. By 1936, the controversial magazine had become very successful and was fondly thought of as the industry bible. Even President Franklin D. Roosevelt had the paper airmailed daily to his desk at the White House."[42]

Wilkerson set his sight beyond that of a prominent magazine publisher—he wanted to be a nightclub proprietor as well. A shrewd businessman, he was aware of two compelling reasons to start new ventures in Hollywood at the onset of The Great Depression. One was his belief that existing establishments for local nightlife were "ordinary." He envisioned extraordinary nightclubs that offered class, sophistication, and ambiance. His second reason was the knowledge that entertainment people from Beverly Hills had money—lots of it—despite the difficult economic times.

Inspiration for his Hollywood ventures came from his New York speakeasy triumphs during Prohibition's 1920s and from his many trips to Europe, where he was fond of spending time in Parisian cafés and nightclubs. Wilkerson's vision of Parisian-styled nightspots became the model for a chain of very profitable Southern California cafés and nightclubs. Though the movie industry dominated Hollywood, the Sunset Strip became the town's glamorous social hub where the stars went to be seen. Wilkerson's enterprises at this time included Ciro's, Café Trocadero, Sunset House, LaRue, and L'Aiglon. These nightspots made him America's most successful nightclub owner and restaurateur.

A COMPULSION TO GAMBLE

Wilkerson suffered from an obsessive-compulsive disorder that manifested itself in many ways, including an addiction to gambling. Despite having lost everything on Black Tuesday, within six months of arriving in California he bet and lost $750,000, and came close to bankruptcy. From craps to poker to horse races, no sum was too large or too small to wager. This compulsive nature—a trait evident in his father—affected every facet of Wilkerson's life, including his smoking three packs of cigarettes and drinking more than a dozen Coca-Colas a day. Most remarkable though, Wilkerson's most compulsive behavior was gambling and regularly risked vast sums of money.

His son wrote in *The Man Who Invented Las Vegas*, "From the moment Wilkerson awoke in the morning he thought of nothing else but gambling. He planned his entire day around the gaming tables and horse tracks. Usually, he would work in the morning and head out for the track in the afternoon. He paid regular visits to Santa Anita or Hollywood Park. He kept a pair of dice in his coat pocket, and a deck of playing cards was never far from reach. At restaurants he would roll the dice on tabletops to determine who picked up the check. Even in his restaurants guests paid if they lost."[43]

Wilkerson could afford to gamble enormous sums because of the various thriving businesses he owned. Three of the most successful were the *Hollywood Reporter,* and his two most popular restaurants, LaRue and Ciro's. The trio grossed a little over one million dollars in annual revenue. After he paid for operating costs and expenses, he was left with about $250,000 a year. Even so, the successful businessman "was led by the same desires that lure every gambler to the felt tables—the dream of easy money."[44]

The publisher often gambled away pre-paid advertising receipts earned by the *Reporter.* When he didn't have access to ready cash, he would write IOUs— casino markers, scores of them. Casino owners regularly extended him extraordinary lines of credit, because they knew he was good for it. "Whatever the amount wagered and lost, Wilkerson had a reputation for honoring his gambling debts." [45]

THE LEGENDARY POKER GAME

Wilkerson regularly played poker at a weekly high stakes game in the Hollywood homes of movie moguls Samuel Goldwyn and Joe Schenck. These games required a minimum of $20,000 buy in and Wilkerson regularly lost thousands a visit. "You had to be rich to gamble that kind of cash at those games," recalled Tom Seward Wilkerson's longtime business partner. "Only the biggies would be there."[46] Invitees were chosen from the highest echelons of Hollywood, including such distinguished men as Darryl Zanuck, Jack Warner, Irving Thalberg, David O. Selznick, and Irving Berlin.

If that wasn't enough, Wilkerson also invited motion picture's well-heeled to his poker games held in the back rooms of the nightclubs he controlled. When the publisher was not playing poker, he tickled his gambling fancy by driving down to Aqua Caliente, a sprawling gaming complex on the Mexican border, where he gambled on everything from table games to horse races. He'd often spend the whole day wagering $12,000 or $15,000 before driving back. During the 1930s Wilkerson also had the opportunity to ride water taxis out beyond the three-mile limit to play table games on illegal gambling ships moored off the California coast, Tony Cornero's SS Rex and the Tango.

Until the late 1930s, Southern California was wide open to gambling and prostitution, but when authorities outlawed these activities in 1938, compulsive gamblers like Wilkerson traveled out of state to seek legal gambling. Consequently, Las Vegas became a favorite gambling setting for Wilkerson. He often chartered a plane in the morning from Los Angeles Municipal Airport to Alamo Airport, today McCarran International. A short cab ride later he'd be playing at the El Rancho Vegas or downtown's El Cortez. Typically, he played a few hours at the tables, winning or losing $20,000 before returning to Hollywood. Distressed at the extent of his losses over the years, and his inability to control his gambling habits, Wilkerson confided in his friend, Joe Schenck, then chairman of 20th Century Fox pictures. Schenck offered a piece of advice that changed Wilkerson's life. "Billy, you need to be on the other side of the table if you're going to endure those kinds of losses. . . . Build a casino. Own the house." Wilkerson realized the wisdom of his friend's advice and thanked him for the insight.

INSPIRATION TO BUILD THE FLAMINGO

In 1944, with Schenck's advice in mind, the beleaguered Hollywood publisher decided to take a more serious look at Las Vegas. Until then, he thought the place served only diehard gamblers like him and lacked the glamour and atmosphere he enjoyed in European venues. The few so-called sawdust joints operating downtown in those days were a far cry from today's casinos. They were saloons that offered a few casino games, such as two or three blackjack tables and perhaps one roulette table.

Wilkerson's first business venture in Vegas came in December 1944 when he arranged to lease the El Rancho Vegas from owner Joe Drown for six months at $50,000. He soon realized that building in Nevada required a more impressive attraction than the modest western-themed El Rancho. More

74

than simply a casino and a hotel, he needed a lavish resort grander in scope to lure the rich movie people from Beverly Hills to the barren desert—something more glamorous than his Hollywood nightclubs. He needed a special resort-hotel.

Though Wilkerson disliked the desert, the town's remote location nevertheless helped induce the troubled gambler into believing Las Vegas could become an ideal site for gambling. Supporting his opportunistic vision was his recognition that a huge market for Las Vegas, hundreds of anxious gamblers like himself lay untouched in Hollywood—resembling an expensive bottle of champagne waiting to be uncorked.

One question puzzled Wilkerson: getting to Las Vegas. He preferred to fly, and had always chartered a plane in his gambling forays to the desert town. But he realized that most of his rich Hollywood clientele enjoyed driving. The visionary publisher decided to take an experimental trip to scout the roads that led to Vegas.

In January 1945, with his Cadillac's trunk loaded with extra gas cans, Wilkerson set out from Los Angeles along California's western edge of Route 66 and headed for Nevada's vast Mojave Desert. He continued through Pasadena, San Bernardino, Victorville, and a few miles northwest of Barstow Wilkerson turned onto Route 91. When the publisher passed through Baker, California, he was near the desert's bottom, almost halfway to Vegas. From there it was mostly uphill to Vegas. He drove the Cadillac windows wide open through searing heat on a dust-ridden, two-lane highway void of rest areas and gas stations. With automobile air-conditioning still a distant fantasy, the almost unendurable inferno was excruciatingly hot. The desert resembled a lunar landscape with blowing sagebrush fading into waves of heat. But this was only January. Wilkerson could only imagine how much hotter the desert would be in mid-summer.

After seven hours of driving some 300 desolate miles, Wilkerson finally rolled down the Sierra Nevada Mountains and into Las Vegas—the nearest legalized gambling location to Hollywood. Without a doubt Wilkerson concluded, it would be asking too much to expect his well-heeled friends and clientele in Beverly Hills to "leave their cozy private card games to brave an arduous drive in grueling weather only to face accommodations and amenities that were, by his standards, totally inadequate."[47]

In late January Wilkerson spotted a for sale sign along Highway 91 a few miles south of downtown Las Vegas. It was a huge 33-acre parcel—on the corner lot were two dilapidated shacks with a faded hotel sign. It belonged to a recently widowed Margaret Folsom, a down-on-her-luck hotel owner who had bought the property for $7,500 only a few months earlier.

Despite his hopeless addiction to gambling, Wilkerson remained a shrewd businessman. To avoid inflating the selling price that might result from rumors of a high roller's interest in Las Vegas property, he hired his attorney, Greg Bautzer to negotiate on his behalf. Within a day, Bautzer managed to nail down a purchase price of $84,000, buying Folsom's property in his name, and waiting nearly a year before registering the deed.

From the beginning, the Hollywood publisher envisioned his future resort as a gambling paradise that would house all his passions under one roof. Furthermore, it had to be unique and outshine the "pedestrian" competition in town. He pictured a desert oasis not only for gamblers, but also for visitors who wanted to relax, who would enjoy a luxurious resort featuring fine dining, floor shows with top-name entertainers, and a variety of outdoor activities.

To put this revelation on paper, in February 1945 he met with architect George Russell and decorator Tom Douglas at his Hollywood office, where he outlined his idea for a central "hub," with the casino as the focal point of a massive complex. Surrounding the casino on the 33-acre property, he wanted to build an indoor shopping mall, glamorous showroom, upscale nightclub, a bar-lounge, several fine restaurants, a café, luxury hotel, and a spa with steam rooms and gym. Outdoor recreation would include a large swimming pool, private bungalows, and handball and tennis courts. Additional features to enhance the sprawling resort included a nine-hole golf course along with a riding stable and a shooting range.

Summing up his casino hub concept, Wilkerson explained the overriding goal to his architect and decorator: to make losing money as simple and as painless as possible for the gambler. His vision was to create an ultra-gambling resort that let players find a total escape in which to "indulge their passion in palatial luxury."[48]

The focus of the complex was the casino—the bread and butter of the expansive facility. Wilkerson wanted a design that funneled hotel guests through the casino at every cross point. With no windows, no wall clocks, and dim overhead lighting, he would ensure that time would pass unnoticed. These elements, he argued, would cloak the true time of day and allow nothing visible to interfere with the total gambling experience.

Wilkerson introduced other radical changes that altered casino design in Las Vegas for years to come. Before 1945, casino game tables had hard edges and typically lacked comfortable seating. Wilkerson believed gaming should be a pleasurable experience, so he ordered rounded edges and cushioned leather padding on all game tables. He also complemented each game with comfortable stools and chairs. His most notable innovation included "air conditioning which would make the Flamingo the first hotel in America with indoor cooling.

Next, he faced the task of choosing a suitable name and logo for his planned casino-resort. Wilkerson usually named his projects long before they were completed. His stylish Hollywood nightclubs had a Parisian flair, and were inspired by his many travels to Europe. In the case of his Las Vegas casino he turned to his love of birds, particularly the beautiful long-legged pink variety he'd encountered during a trip to Florida. To develop an appropriate logo he turned to Hollywood graphic artist Bert Worth.

ENTER GUS GREENBAUM AND MOE SEDWAY

Wilkerson had gained a lot of business expertise running the *Hollywood Reporter* and his various upscale nightspots. Despite his success in those endeavors, he knew managing an immense casino complex was an entirely different undertaking. Although a gambler by nature, he understood little about the inner workings of a gambling establishment. In his determination to create a successful high-class casino, he knew he needed professionals with experience in casino management.

Wilkerson turned for help to Gus Greenbaum and Moe Sedway, owners of the El Cortez Casino, who had developed a good reputation for operating table games. In the mid 1940s, Las Vegas casino owners typically farmed out gaming operations to independent contractors adept in certain functions. For a silent partnership and a percentage of the gaming profits, these two men agreed to manage Wilkerson's Flamingo casino and be completely responsible for every phase of its operation. In addition, they agreed to help procure all required gaming licenses. At first glance, the arrangement appeared to be a great partnership. Although Greenbaum and Sedway lacked Wilkerson's panache for developing a glamorous business, they knew everything there was to know about the successful operation of a casino.

The original estimate to build the Flamingo came in at one million dollars. Of that, Wilkerson had already spent about $200,000 from the building fund on architectural plans and site acquisition. In the interim, as the first phase of construction began, Wilkerson continued to gamble at the El Cortez. Unfortunately, his gambling losses and debts to Moe Sedway totaled $400,000 at this time, which eventually had to be paid from the building fund, and would leave him with only a balance of $400,000.

With characteristic confidence, Wilkerson decided to get the losses back at Sedway's El Cortez. In April 1945, he risked $200,000 at the gaming tables, only to lose it all. Now he was down to $200,000 remaining in the building fund.

All the same, in November 1945 contractors broke ground on the Flamingo. Within six weeks, with nearly a third of the resort's construction complete, Wilkerson ran into more troubles. The project's construction budget had ballooned to just under $1.2 million—$200,000 over the original estimate—a shortfall that Wilkerson did not have.

To make up for the deficit, Wilkerson once again tried his luck at the gaming tables. Taking $150,000 of the remaining $200,000 in construction funds, he confidently risked it at the gaming tables. Once again he lost everything.

With most of his construction funding gone, Wilkerson became desperate. He tried to convince several Hollywood studio heads to donate materials from their back lots, but to no avail. What little he did receive barely helped in the overall construction effort. At one point, Wilkerson got additional funding from his friend Howard Hughes who owned several film-related businesses, and had an annual advertising account with the *Reporter*. Under the guise that it was a year's pre-paid advertising, Hughes advanced Wilkerson the funds without question. But the troubled gambler lost this money too.

By January of 1946, Wilkerson's cash amounted to less than $50,000. No one would lend him money. Construction of his dream resort ground to a standstill. Distraught, and with no one to turn to, he paid everyone at the construction site in cash and virtually abandoned the unfinished Flamingo.

In the 1940s Wilkerson lacked the financial resources of modern casino developers, because in those days banks refused to lend money to build casinos. Once Wilkerson's compulsive gambling sapped his bankroll, he had very few options to replenish his construction funding. These were the days before Valley Bank expedited loans from the Teamsters Pension Fund before Wall Street and corporate America solicited the public to purchase gaming stock, and before Michael Milken created junk-bond financing, which in 1989 financed construction of Steve Wynn's Mirage. Before these investment sources existed, there was only the Mafia with its suitcases full of illicit cash.

A month passed. The shell of a partially constructed Flamingo rested in the arid desert—its steel girders standing erect like a flesh-picked skeleton in the midst of a 33- acre western ghost town. With the Hollywood publisher at the end of his financial rope, Moe Sedway brought Wilkerson's idle project to the attention of East Coast Mob boss Meyer Lansky. Sedway saw the financially troubled Flamingo as a marvelous opportunity for his syndicate pals to expand their Las Vegas operations.

At first, Lansky failed to share Sedway's optimism about Las Vegas. Lansky believed the Flamingo's setting—a remote site where summer temperatures soared to well over 100° F—was too inhospitable to attract crowds of high rollers. The New Yorker's skepticism began to fade when Sedway described, in vivid detail, Wilkerson's dream of a lavish air-conditioned resort. As Lansky visualized how huge sums of money could be earned in air-cooled comfort, he decided to finance the Flamingo's completion.

The scheme was carefully thought out and set in motion.

81

Someone unknown to Wilkerson would make him an offer he couldn't refuse. That February, Wilkerson and the builder, Bud Raulston were touring the ghostly building site when a well-dressed middle-aged businessman drove up to the pair. He got out of the car, approached the two men, and introduced himself as G. Harry Rothberg from New York City. Rothberg informed Wilkerson that his firm was capable of funding the necessary money to complete the project and proposed to provide $1 million up front. The contractual agreement gave Wilkerson creative freedom and stipulated that when the Flamingo opened, not later than March 1, 1947, Wilkerson would become sole general manager. In exchange for financing, Wilkerson would hold a one-third share in the project: all others would be silent partners.

Wilkerson thanked Rothberg for the offer and told him he would give it serious consideration. At this point Wilkerson felt he was out of options. He'd already thought of abandoning the project altogether. He had no problem with the idea of investors, especially silent ones who took a piece of the action without getting involved with operations. Overall, Wilkerson found the offer acceptable, except for one aspect. At his second meeting with Rothberg a few days later, Wilkerson negotiated for an additional contractual condition—title to the land would be held exclusively in his name. Rothberg agreed, and by March 1946 a contract was signed between Rothberg and Wilkerson. Soon after, $1 million was made available and construction resumed on the Flamingo.

Within a month, three men drove onto the construction

site in a fancy, late-model car. Wilkerson immediately recognized two of the men: Gus Greenbaum and Moe Sedway, the silent partners who had agreed to run the casino. They brought with them a well-dressed man who boldly introduced himself as the publisher's new partner in the Flamingo. The audacious individual was none other than Meyer Lansky's Mob enforcer, the infamous Ben Siegel.

THE SIEGEL/WILKERSON PARTNERSHIP

Meyer Lansky's choice of Ben Siegel to oversee his Las Vegas interests seemed a natural liaison. Wilkerson already knew Siegel, who patronized his nightclubs, and they lived near each other in Beverly Hills.

In the beginning the partnership went smoothly. The two worked together out of Wilkerson's office. The usually aggressive and brash gangster became remarkably useful, followed Wilkerson's guidance, and learned as much as he could from the ground up about building a multi-faceted resort. Siegel was particularly helpful at gathering black market building materials

through his underworld connections in California. But things soon went awry.

For whatever reason, Siegel, the gangster with a hair-trigger temper, started acting like his old self, playing the role of big shot. Instead of the pupil following the tutelage of his mentor, Siegel began making decisions without consulting Wilkerson. His behavior seemed filled with paranoia and resentment, as when he changed the architectural plans and informed the construction workers that Wilkerson had promoted him to boss. Taking credit for Wilkerson's vision, Siegel went so far as to claim that the Flamingo was his own idea. Although he apologized whenever Wilkerson grew angry, Siegel kept demanding more involvement in the project.

Wilkerson compromised by allowing Siegel to oversee the hotel, while he retained the upper hand with everything else. But things became further disorganized when Siegel asked to have his own architect and builder. The result was total mayhem, as two distinct management spheres functioned within one complex with no communication between them. Matters came to a head when Siegel's unbridled greed and extravagance overspent the budget allotted. He went to Wilkerson for more money, but that was denied.

In May 1946, Siegel decided the original agreement between Wilkerson and Rothberg had been a mistake. Instead, Siegel wanted sole operational control of the Flamingo. To buy out Wilkerson's creative input, Siegel offered Wilkerson five percent more stock participation and formed a new corporation, naming himself as president and taking control of all operations. Now Siegel was the largest principal stockholder, all other partners, including Wilkerson became mere shareholders. From then on, the Flamingo functioned as a Mob-run operation, with Siegel at the helm.

Siegel wasted no time putting his own plans into action. Never again would he consult with Wilkerson. He fired all of Wilkerson's on-site affiliates and staff. The original architect and decorator were discharged and Del Webb and Richard Stadelman were awarded the jobs. Responsibility for interior decorations was given to the gangster's girlfriend, the notorious Virginia Hill.

SIEGEL'S TAKEOVER OF THE FLAMINGO

In the period following the end of World War II, the scarcity of building materials not only inflated the Flamingo's budget, it incurred other problems when Siegel got involved in making a lot of "interesting" changes in the project's building plans: changes that conflicted with blueprints Wilkerson, the man in charge at the time, had already approved.

Siegel's design changes to the Flamingo were not only extravagant but also ludicrous. For example, he intended to provide each room with its own sewer system at a cost of over one million dollars. That change required the purchase of new toilets ($50,000) and a new boiler (an additional $113,000). A change in kitchen design costing $29,000 could be considered relatively modest on the scale at which Siegel operated. These extravagant, exorbitant costs testified to Siegel's troubled mind. The four-story Flamingo was built like a fortified vault, with reinforced concrete walls poured around heavy-duty steel stolen from naval shipyards. Siegel's rooftop suite was built with trap doors and escape hatches; one reportedly led to a getaway car in his private garage. "There were gun portals and hallways leading to nowhere."[49] By the time the Flamingo finally opened its doors, it was virtually "a physical manifestation of Siegel's inherent fears," cited the *Las Vegas Review-Journal*.

As if these cost overruns weren't bad enough, Siegel's lack

of oversight resulted in substantial thefts of building materials and supplies. Many of the pilfered supplies were sold back to the project the following day. The World War II shortage of steel and other crucial building supplies drove cost overruns even higher. By the time of the Flamingo's completion in 1947, the cost of the project had escalated to $6 million, a phenomenal overrun of $5 million.

The first sign of trouble for Siegel came in November of 1946, when the syndicate dons issued an ultimatum; provide an accounting of expenditures or forfeit funding. Producing some kind of budget for the boys was the last thing Siegel wanted to do. Alas, how does one justify spending $6 million for a project originally budgeted at $1 million, perhaps $1.5 million, tops?

When Siegel realized he could be in serious danger, he tried to raise money by selling nonexistent stock in the Flamingo. Then he hurried to finish construction by doubling his on-site work force, believing the project could be completed in half the time. The Mobster-turned-inept-project manager paid overtime and double-time. He even offered bonuses tied to performance deadlines, hoping to increase productivity. A second money-raising scheme involved moving the opening up from the original date of March 1, 1947, to December 26, 1946, in hopes of earning enough money from casino profits to cover construction costs and begin paying dividends to investors.

The Flamingo's opening turned out to be a huge flop. After two weeks in operation the gaming tables were $275,000 in the red. As a result Siegel finally shut down the entire complex in late January. Meanwhile, Meyer Lansky persuaded his syndicate pals back in New York to grant a reprieve, which gave an extension to his lifelong pal. With Siegel getting yet another chance, he reopened the Flamingo in March as originally planned and made an effort to turn things around.

In the interim, the dons back east grew impatient for a more immediate return on their investment. The situation got worse when Lansky learned that Siegel's girlfriend Virginia Hill had access to the Flamingo building fund and frequently flew to Switzerland to make large cash deposits into a numbered Swiss bank account.

Meanwhile, a few strings were still left untied by the self-appointed president of the Flamingo. Most crucial was ownership of the 33-acre parcel of land. According to the original contract with Rothberg, Wilkerson was one-third owner of the project and sole owner of the land. Siegel was not satisfied, as he wanted control of the land too. He offered Wilkerson an additional five percent shareholder stake in exchange for title to the land. They negotiated, and Wilkerson granted land ownership to Siegel for ten percent more in stock. As a result, in August 1946, Wilkerson held a 48 percent share in the Flamingo Corporation making him its largest single shareholder.

THE ILL-FATED STOCKHOLDER MEETING

In December 1946, Wilkerson received a phone call from the Director of the FBI, J. Edgar Hoover warning him about Ben Siegel. Unfortunately, the call came too late. Wilkerson had too much involved in the Flamingo to remove himself without endangering his investment. To protect himself and his interests,

Wilkerson decided to make the best of a very bad situation. He hired a press agent, and the two began developing a significant publicity campaign to make sure the outside world became aware of the Flamingo. The campaign would focus on the property's gala opening in December 1946, and on the hotel's extravagant cost, which Wilkerson placed at $5 million. In that way Wilkerson would alert The Mob to Siegel's over-spending and possible skimming. In the midst of the publicity campaign, Siegel held a stockholder's meeting at the unfinished hotel. Present at the meeting were Wilkerson, his attorney Greg Bautzer, along with Gus Greenbaum and Moe Sedway. Representing Ben Siegel were Louis Wiener, his legal counsel, and Clifford Jones the Lieutenant Governor of the State of Nevada at that time.

At the meeting, Siegel proceeded in true Mob fashion, demanding Wilkerson hand over his ownership shares free and clear. After learning Siegel had oversold shares of Flamingo stock, thereby driving down the price, Wilkerson's attorney refused. Siegel flew into one of his psychotic rages and threatened to kill Wilkerson.

Prior to this meeting, Wilkerson had ignored the gangster's nasty occupation and killer reputation. Now, however, Siegel's true persona came to haunt him, and Wilkerson feared for his life. To further ensure his safety, Wilkerson took the first flight to New York, where he boarded a ship bound for France. From the port of Le Havre he drove to Paris and booked a room in an upscale hotel under an assumed name. Only a trusted few knew of his whereabouts. Wilkerson planned to wait it out until Siegel's partners learned of his extravagant spending and his overselling of

Flamingo stock. Wilkerson expected them to eventually fire Siegel, leading to a change in management, and Wilkerson would be reinstated as creative director. Then, he would finally be able to complete his dream resort.

THE FLAMINGO OPENS

The gala opening of the Flamingo on December 26, 1946 was a star-studded affair. Band leader Xavier Cugat provided the music. Celebrity guests included Rose Marie, George Jessel, George Raft, Joan Crawford, Clark Gable, and Lana Turner. Jimmy Durante headlined the entertainment. The splashy opening unfortunately bombed due to poor timing. The day after Christmas is typically a very slow day for Las Vegas, and it rained that day. The other problem was the hotel's still unfinished construction left the guests with nowhere to stay.

When Meyer Lansky learned of the Flamingo's weak opening, he convinced the other syndicate bosses to give Siegel more time to operate the resort. By January 1947, however, the lack of business forced Siegel to close the Flamingo until construction on the hotel could be completed. Through all this, Wilkerson had held onto his hope that the Flamingo's Mob investors would eventually refuse to allow the hotel's ownership to remain in the hands of a psychopath. Yet once the Flamingo closed, Wilkerson realized he needed to get out from under, so he offered to sell his share for $2 million, with a stipulation absolving him of further obligations and responsibility—including financial.

Despite the still unfinished construction of the hotel, the Flamingo reopened in March 1947 to a different result. Within two months the resort earned a $250,000 profit, allowing Lansky to point out to the boys that his lifelong friend Ben Siegel was, after all, correct in his belief about Las Vegas.

On March 19 both Siegel and Rothberg signed a legal document that totally absolved Wilkerson from any wrongdoing in the Flamingo Corporation. He was to receive partial payment of $300,000 in early May, with the balance due in ninety days. Within a week of the signing, the publisher received a frightening phone call from an anonymous woman. Frantic, she told Wilkerson her recently paroled husband had been contracted to kill him. Wilkerson must have taken the warning seriously because he immediately headed back to Paris. Soon, his daily Trade View column for the *Reporter* was by-lined from the French capital.

While in Paris, Wilkerson received a call from his manager, George Kennedy, telling him of a message from an unknown person who said his client needed to stay in Paris "until this is over."[50] Kennedy claimed to have no knowledge of the meaning or origin of the strange message. Less than a month later, on the morning of June 21, Wilkerson bought his newspaper, sat down at a sidewalk café, and ordered a Coke. When he unfolded the paper, he saw the article telling of Ben Siegel's death. Immediately he returned to his hotel to pack his bags, and within 48 hours Wilkerson flew back to Los Angeles.

On June 25 police came to Wilkerson's Hollywood office making inquiries into Siegel's death. The detectives questioned him about his partnership in the Flamingo, insinuating that Wilkerson knew more than he was telling them. "They implied a direct link between the publisher and organized crime based on association stemming from his involvement in the project,"[51] said George Kennedy in a later interview. Wilkerson categorically denied any links to organized crime or wrongdoing whatsoever.

SIEGEL'S DEMISE

On the night of June 20, 1947, two men sat quietly in Virginia Hill's Beverly Hills mansion at 810 North Linden Drive. One of them, Ben Siegel, was reading the *Los Angeles Times;* the other was his associate, syndicate conduit Alan Smiley. Siegel's girlfriend had flown to Europe a few days earlier. Suddenly, an unknown assailant fired nine shots through a window with a .30-caliber M1 carbine. Four shots entered Siegel's body, killing him almost instantly—two shots to the head, and two through the lungs. Smiley was unharmed in the assault. No suspects were ever charged in the murder, and the crime remains officially unsolved.

The Los Angeles Coroner's Report stated that Siegel's death was caused by cerebral hemorrhage. Remarkably, though, the pressure created by a bullet's striking and passing through Siegel's skull blew his left eye out of its socket. According to author Anthony Bruno, "Siegel was actually *not* shot exactly through the eye (the eyeball would have been destroyed if this had been the case), the bullet-through-the-eye style of killing, nevertheless became popular in Mafia lore and in movies."[52]

Siegel's high Hollywood profile undoubtedly became an embarrassment to the boys back east. He was frequently seen with such major silver screen stars as Cary Grant and everyone's favorite gangster portrayer, George Raft. George Raft once said of his pal "He was a frustrated actor and secretly wanted a movie career, but he never quite had nerve enough to ask for a part in one of my pictures."[53]

The order to kill Siegel came down because he'd committed more than one major sin. He'd lost money for The Mob, stolen money from The Mob, and brought publicity to The Mob, whose members preferred to keep a low profile. His murder showcased Las Vegas as the Mecca of underworld gambling. To paraphrase Wallace Turner's book *Gambler's Money*, "The Mob arrived in Vegas and The Mob stayed."[54]

But others knew Bugsy as an intense individual who harbored a charitable streak. He was a soft touch for the Damon Runyon Cancer Fund. His employees at the Flamingo thought well of him. He was good to them, and a lot of tears were shed when he was killed.

Still others knew Siegel as a textbook paranoid, always on edge, who, according to Don Garvin, the Flamingo's chief engineer, insisted on changing the locks of his room at the Flamingo every other week. Unable to trust Gavin to the task, Siegel and his then girlfriend Virginia Hill would watch from the hallway as the locksmith worked.

Yet no amount of caution prevented the boys from disciplining one of their own. In the end, Ben Siegel emerged as an immortal Las Vegas legend. Ben Siegel's involvement with the Flamingo inevitably was the cause of his gruesome demise, and linked the dashing psychopath forever with the fortunes of Las Vegas.

What Billy Wilkerson started and Siegel's successors completed were two different entities. The Flamingo's new management team under Gus Greenbaum favored a more middle class ambiance. For instance, they departed from Wilkerson's vision of mandatory black tie in the upscale restaurants, and formal attire in the casino. In a 1972 interview, Greg Bautzer made the following observation: "Under the new partnership, the Flamingo became a non-exclusive facility—an egalitarian establishment where gamblers could relax and flirt elegantly with Lady Luck at prices affordable to almost anyone."[55] Greenbaum's management team also made the Flamingo very successful, earning a profit of $4 million in the first year alone.

* * *

WHEREABOUTS OF VIRGINIA HILL

Minutes after Ben Siegel's death, Gus Greenbaum and Moe Sedway showed up at the Flamingo and informed Miss Hill of her lover's death, telling her they were taking over the Flamingo.

Afterwards, Hill flew back to Europe where she lived her remaining years. Whether she returned the embezzled $2 million to Meyer Lansky is unclear, although the film *Bugsy* makes it appear that she did. Actually, she most likely did repay the stolen money. If she hadn't The Mob would surely not have allowed her to live.

During the final years of her life, separated from her husband, Virginia Hill was supported by her only child Peter Hauser, who worked as a restaurant waiter.

That Hill needed financial support gives even more credence to the theory that she returned the embezzled $2 million to Lansky.

EARLY LIFE

Born in 1916 in Alabama, Virginia Hill—aka "the Flamingo," so-named for her long legs—was already a beauty in the 1930s when she moved to Marietta, Georgia, with her mother and two brothers. She left home at 17 and moved to Chicago, taking a job as a dancer at the World's Fair and working as a waitress on the side. At the restaurant she met the first mobster in her life—Joseph Epstein, Al Capone's accountant. Soon the two were sleeping together and working together in his bookmaking business.

While in Chicago, she became the mistress of one gangster after another, all members of the Capone outfit including Frank Nitti, Joe Adonis, Charles Fischetti, Frank Costello and Major Riddle. The sassy, sharp-tongued Georgia peach managed to keep her status on the A-list of underworld women while she stood toe-to-toe with many of Capone's cronies, and eventually Ben Siegel.

Hill's relationships with the Chicago Outfit were short-lived. She set her sights on Hollywood and left for Los Angeles, intending to use her Mob connections to become a star of the silver screen. Instead, the long-legged beauty met and fell in love with Ben Siegel.

Virginia Hill and Ben Siegel became acquainted through Joe Adonis in 1937 at a restaurant in New York City. It was only a one-night stand, but they rekindled their relationship later at a party in New York in 1939. After that the pair became inseparable. They fell in love, and as their relationship evolved, they fought as hard as they loved. Both were known for having a short fuse. Remarkably, Hill was one of the few people who dared stand up to Siegel when he went berserk.

Yet, even before Hill met Siegel, she was one of the select few women entrusted with Mafia secrets. She was allegedly a courier for the Chicago Outfit, a charge she denied during the 1950-51 Kefauver Hearings.

During those hearings, Charles W. Tobey the Senator from New Hampshire, became curious about the reason so many men had given Virginia Hill so much money. He made the mistake of asking about her income. He had information there was a doctor in Chicago, Joe Epstein from the Capone Mob, two gangsters from New York, Joey Adonis and Ben Siegel, a millionaire in Mexico, and a New York concert violinist—all giving her money over the years, for no apparent reason.

According to author Steve Fischer from *When The Mob Ran Vegas*, Hill's official testimony went like this:

SENATOR TOBEY: Why would Joe Epstein give you all that money, Miss Hill?

WITNESS: You really want to know?

SENATOR TOBEY: Yes, I really want to know.

WITNESS: Then I'll tell you why. Because I'm the best cocksucker in town!

According to observers, Hill's crude reply left the entire committee speechless and shocked television viewers across the country. **SENATOR KEFAUVER:** Order! I demand order! [56]

Bea Sedway, the wife of Moe Sedway and a friend of both Hill and Siegel, said that when it came to informing on The Mob, "She was smart and she knew how to keep her mouth shut."[57]

Fifteen years after she testified in front of the Kefauver Committee, in March 1966, Virginia Hill died at the age of 49 of an apparent overdose of sleeping pills in Koppl, near Salzburg, Austria. Her body was found near an uninhabited area, near a bridge spanning a small stream called the Alterbach.

Historians offer two competing theories about the death of Virginia Hill. The first of these is that she was depressed about her life circumstances, swallowed a bottle of sleeping pills, walked outdoors, and lay down in the cold to die. The second possibility involves a visit paid to Hill two days before her death by her former paramour, Mob hit man Joe Adonis. According to this theory, either The Mob finally caught up with her and meted out justice for her role in helping Siegel steal their money, or they killed her because she tried to shake down Adonis for money by threatening to tell the world what she knew about Mob activities.

THE FLAMINGO LEGACY

With Siegel's demise Billy Wilkerson figured the Flamingo debacle was finally over. But unfortunately, he was dreadfully wrong. Not unlike a chronic sore that never heals, a horrible reminder of his partnership with Ben Siegel occurred in 1950. According to Wilkerson's bride-to-be, Beatrice Noble in January of that year she and Billy drove to Sun Valley, Idaho for a week's stay. Noble described in an interview the incident that happened that day; during an evening meal in a busy upscale restaurant, Virginia Hill entered the room and spotted Billy. "She hurried over to his table and exploded with anger reminiscent of Benny's rages."[58]

"It's all your fault you lousy prick!" Hill screamed at the publisher. "It was because of you they killed him!"[59]

Conversations in the restaurant gradually fell to a slight murmur and people stopped eating, turning their attention to the outburst as Hill lambasted Wilkerson accusing him of being responsible for her boyfriend's death. Hill sincerely believed that the timing of Siegel's death had been accelerated by his inability to procure the publisher's stock in the Flamingo.

Noble went on to describe Hill's rude behavior in

the midst of what was supposed to be a pleasurable dining experience. Hill had worked herself up into a mad frenzy screaming at the top of her lungs for what seemed minutes by Noble's estimate, finally "slapping Wilkerson's face violently back and forth several times and stormed out of the restaurant."

"The entire room went quiet," remembered Wilkerson's fiancé. "After she left you could have heard a pin drop."

"Billy Wilkerson never saw Virginia Hill again. For him, this was the last physical remnant of the Flamingo debacle."[60]

Billy Wilkerson's addictions included being a workaholic, and its ramifications afflicted his personal life, leading to five divorces. Yet it was his sixth wife, Beatrice Noble as well as fatherhood that inspired him to quit the habits that had besieged him all his life. In his sixth decade, with the birth of his son in October 1951, he finally quit gambling and settled down, enjoying a stable and happy family relationship. Billy Wilkerson continued to head the *Hollywood Reporter* and write his daily Trade View column until his death in September 1962. He was 71.

In a closing note, W.R. Wilkerson III writes, "To date, history has failed Wilkerson. He is the quintessential victim of myth. During his lifetime, Wilkerson enjoyed enormous celebrity status. For three decades, practically everyone in Hollywood knew him, or of him. Yet a mere thirty years after his death Billy

Wilkerson is practically unknown."[61] Billy Wilkerson's reluctance to openly claim authorship of the Flamingo helped nurture the Bugsy myth. Today only a few morsels of evidence still exist which tie Wilkerson to the Flamingo. The truth is buried even deeper when Hollywood re-writes history producing powerful feature films. "It is as if history suffers from Alzheimer's and like a sleeping Rip Van Winkle, must be awakened, or, in drastic cases like Wilkerson's, vigorously resuscitated."[62]

* * *

Chapter 6

MICKEY COHEN: HOLLYWOOD'S CELEBRITY GANGSTER

*a*s the 1890s gave way to the early 1900s, a surge of Jewish immigrants fled the poverty, harsh climate, and anti Semitism experienced in pre-revolutionary Russia and made their way to the sanctuary of America's shores. Part of that surge was the poor and uneducated parents of Mickey Cohen, Max and Fanny. Unable to speak the language, the couple settled in a ghetto neighborhood of Brownsville, Brooklyn, New York.

By the time Meyer Harris—called Mickey—was born into the Cohen family on September 4, 1913, he was the youngest of six children; with three brothers and two sisters. Hardly into his thirties, tragedy struck when Max died of an unknown cause two months after Mickey's birth, leaving Fanny burdened with six young children and little else.

In 1915, while her four oldest children stayed with relatives, Fanny brought a barely two-year-old Mickey and his four-year-old sister Lillian along in a courageous move to Los Angeles, America's fastest growing city. Their precise destination was Boyle Heights, situated on a bluff two miles east of downtown, and populated by a working class blend of mostly Eastern European Jews, Mexicans and Italians. Los Angeles was home to the largest Jewish population west of Chicago, renowned for its rich and glamorous movie industry and the extraordinarily wealthy Jews who ruled Hollywood; conversely, Boyle Heights was looked down on as the city's Jewish slum.

Author Tere Tereba writes, "A tiny woman who spoke little English, Fanny Cohen was accustomed to a harsh existence and adversity. She had experienced the dangerous odyssey from her native Kiev to New York, her young husband's death, and her difficult journey across America to the Pacific coast."[63] Settling into a two story stucco apartment house at 131 N. Breed Street,

Fanny opened a small neighborhood grocery nearby. As the money began coming in, she sent for her four older children.

With his mother working long hours at the store, and deficient of a father's influence, Mickey was without adequate parental supervision. Eleven years his elder it was Mickey's brother Harry who became his stand-in father and corrupting influence. When he was five years old, each day his brothers would drop him off at the busy corner of Brooklyn and Soto, the hub of Boyle Heights' commercial district. There little Mickey, legs dangling, sat on a stack of newspapers hawking the *Los Angeles Record* at five cents a copy.

By the time he was six years old brother Harry had exposed Mickey to gambling and bootlegging during late-night forays to underworld speakeasys, the gin mills that had sprung up in the early 1920s, though young Mickey mostly slept in the car. These were the early years of Prohibition, when Harry taught Mickey how to make gin in the back of the store, all while mother Cohen, a natural survivalist, turned a blind eye to her boys' chicanery.

As the years rolled on school fell by the wayside while Mickey spent most of his time peddling newspapers on downtown street corners. He also frequented the local pool halls passing bets and selling bootleg liquor to local hustlers. Mickey's first run in with the law occurred at age eight, when Prohibition officers nabbed him at the illegal still in the back of the family store. He was interned at juvenile hall for bootlegging, but after only serving a few hours he was released. Mickey would later boast that his first offense was fixed by his brother Louis' political connections.

Soon thereafter Mickey, armed with a baseball bat, was apprehended trying to rob the box office of the Columbia, a downtown theater. For that crime he spent seven months of his tenth year incarcerated in reform school.

After his release, Mickey began peddling newspapers in the heart of downtown L.A where his penchant for fighting earned him first-rate locations as a street vendor. Mickey's toughness gave him the ability to fend off other newsboys who challenged him for the rights to prime corners. In fact, he became such a good fighter that other street vendors often hired Mickey for protection.

Though small in stature and hard-hitting in a downtown fight, Mickey Cohen had a natural warm sense of humor and a generous nature, and was well-liked by the kids living in his Boyle Heights environs. The neighborhood children—the Jews, Mexicans, and Italians—all got along. "But it wasn't until later that Mickey began boxing at the L.A. Coliseum and the Olympic Auditorium that Mickey first heard racial slurs. 'If anyone called someone a kike, spic or wop in our neighborhood, we would beat his head in,'" [64] he explained.

Then through a friend, Mickey was introduced to Abe Roth, a respected local sports figure and boxing referee. Under Roth's tutelage, Mickey the street brawler began learning the sport of boxing under the Queensberry's rules. In his 11th year Mickey started boxing in three-round amateur bouts around metropolitan L.A., winning most of them. He fought almost every night, and as he progressed his confidence grew. By age 13 Mickey won his first title, the city's flyweight division of the American Legion

Newsboy's Championship.

Four years later, on April 8, 1930, at the age of 17 Mickey fought in his first professional fight against Patsy Farr in Cleveland, Ohio. His biggest challenge though, came on June 12, 1931, when Mickey fought and lost the match against World Featherweight Champion Tommy Paul, having been knocked out after 2:20 into the first round. His last professional fight was on May 14, 1933 against Baby Arizmendi in Tijuana, Baja Mexico.

While he struggled with his professional boxing career, Mickey Cohen moved to Chicago in Prohibition's later years joining the Capone Outfit as an enforcer. During this period, Cohen was arrested in the deaths of several gangsters in the robbery of a poker game that went awry. After serving a brief sentence in prison, Cohen was released and rejoined The Outfit under Jake Guzik, running card games and other illegal operations. After an argument with a rival gambler Cohen was forced to flee Chicago and relocated in Cleveland.

COHEN AND SIEGEL OUT WEST

With little work for the ex-prizefighter in Cleveland, Lou Rothkopf with orders from his close associate Meyer Lansky, sent Mickey Cohen to Los Angeles to join up with Ben Siegel. After the Flamingo opened, Cohen managed the sports book and helped implement Siegel's race and wire service there and in Mob-run casinos in Las Vegas.

As their relationship evolved, together Cohen and Siegel became an effective extension of the East Coast Syndicate. Working jointly, they became very successful at expanding organized crime in the West beyond the antiquated small-time operations that existed under the old Sicilian styled Moustache Petes into the multi-million-dollar criminal empire that controlled gambling, narcotics, politics and the film industry unions.

Even though Mickey Cohen and Ben Siegel became close friends and shared similar interests, in many ways they were completely opposite of each other. In fact, Cohen was a mere shadow of his new gangster friend. Siegel was tall, handsome, well-spoken, polished and friends with several Hollywood celebrities, including film star George Raft. Out on the town Siegel socialized with Hollywood's elite, "courted royalty and bedded starlets while his shadow Mickey was picking their pockets, robbing their safes and breaking their bones."[65] They were both ruthless, violent men who enjoyed the same things: beautiful women, fine clothes, and luxurious cars. Siegel, though, in public was able to conceal his dark side and project a more sociable personality, Cohen was what he was. He was illiterate, loud, and boisterous and made no apologies for his lifestyle and lack of sophistication.

After Ben Siegel was killed in 1947 supposedly for his involvement in the Flamingo debacle, which included stealing syndicate money from its building fund, Mickey Cohen flourished as the syndicate's West Coast emissary and enforcer.

"If any gangster personified The Mob in Los Angeles, it was Mickey Cohen. He loved the spotlight, and if it wasn't focused on him, he would seek it out,"[66] as transcribed from a *Mob Attraction* exhibit. The well-dressed and dapper Cohen— owned his own clothing store which gave him access to a large selection of custom suits—was often seen with beautiful women in many of Hollywood's finest restaurants. Though Mickey Cohen was a small, pudgy man, his taste in clothing and home décor were big and extravagant. All his dress clothes had "Mickey" stitched onto the underlining, while his residence was furnished with the finest money could buy. Around his house Cohen's favorite things were toy clowns and bulldogs. The clown statuettes were there simply to amuse him, while the presence of a pet bulldog exemplified how he saw himself: short in stature, yet tough as nails.

Mickey Cohen's public image as a dapper celebrity gangster tends to give people a false impression of the under-sized gangster. Beneath that smiling and amiable persona was a man with a notorious underworld reputation as a tough and violent Mob enforcer.

For protection Cohen hired tough guy Johnny Stompanatoto to serve as his bodyguard. The tall, handsome, and charming Stompanatoto easily blended in with the Hollywood crowd. He dated the beautiful actress Lana Turner, and in public the couple seemed all smiles. Behind the scenes, however, it was a different, ugly story. Stompanatoto was physically abusive to Turner, although few people were aware of it. One who did know of the abuse of Turner was her daughter, Cheryl Crane, who one night in defense of her mother stabbed Stompanatoto to death.

Cheryl Crane was indicted for murder and eventually acquitted of the charge. Stompanatoto's family, however, successfully sued Turner in civil court. In a very generous gesture, Mickey Cohen paid the defendant's legal fees. Ironically though, and to Miss Turner's utmost displeasure, in the end Cohen sold the prized love letters of Turner to Stompanato to the press so he could recoup his expenditures spent in court.

"When rival gangster Jack Dragna inadvertently destroyed Cohen's wardrobe in a failed attempt to blow up his home, it was hard to tell what upset Cohen more: the attempt on his life or the loss of his suits," noted The Mob *Attraction*. Cohen soon converted his Brentwood home into a fortress, installing alarm systems, flood lights, and a well-supplied arsenal kept, as he often quipped, next to his 200 custom-made suits.

LATER YEARS

By 1947, Mickey Cohen had become one of Southern California's most prominent underworld figures, as the media labeled him L.A.'s Al Capone. He was now 35, and at this point in his life had already managed to survive—either through luck or ineptness of the assassins—five attempts on his life from opposing gangsters. Standing five-foot-five in his custom made elevator shoes, the cunning, ruthless former prizefighter was now as much a part of Southern California as movie stars, Mexicans, and gridlock traffic. Mickey's underworld exploits—the numerous assassination attempts on his life, the alleged hits attributed to him that made it appear he was getting away with murder— became the fodder for news reporters. Having grown into a figure of immense fascination with the public, virtually everything Cohen did became front-page news. As such, the flamboyant Mickey Cohen became the flash point of an ongoing L.A. mob war and major political upheaval. Thus, the local reporters in search of a good crime story trailed him everywhere.

1947 was also the same year Mickey was scheduled to appear before a grand jury investigating police corruption. It was because of this grand jury investigation the LAPD, political figures, and members of the underworld, even certain members of his gang, all wanted Cohen dead.

After a night out on the town, at about 2:00 in the morning Mickey Cohen arrived at Sherry's, his favorite after-hour hangout on the famed Sunset Strip. Impeccably dressed in his custom light grey suit and matching wide-brimmed fedora, he entered the smoke-filled restaurant at 9039 Sunset Boulevard. By the time he sat down at his favorite booth #12 at the rear, back to the wall, Mickey was surrounded by reporters. Some had been tailing him—others were simply waiting for Hollywood's celebrity gangster to show up, as it was no secret where Mickey liked to hang in the early morning hours.

Soon after he had ordered his usual, two scoops of chocolate ice cream, he turned his attention to the reporters and began kibitzing with them in his brash style of street-wise hoodlum slang. Florabel Muir, a veteran newswoman who Mickey was familiar with, asked him if it was dangerous to be out clubbing. "Not as long as you people are around," the mobster told her. "Even a crazy man wouldn't take a chance shooting where a reporter might get hit." Knocking wood, he added, "You're too hot."[67]

At 4 a.m. plans for Mickey Cohen's exit began. Near the front door were two plainclothes police men. Because Cohen was such a crucial witness in the upcoming grand jury investigation, one of them, Harry Cooper, had recently been assigned by

California's attorney general as Cohen's bodyguard. As Cohen walked thru the restaurant he had reporters all around him. Cooper saw him coming and peaked out the front door, then turned back to Cohen giving him the all clear signal. Cohen, accompanied by a phalanx of police and reporters, moved through the door and out onto the neon-lit Strip. Muir had cautiously lagged behind. Moments after the group were outside, Muir heard gun fire—bang, bang, bang—what she witnessed next was horrifying.

A short distance from the door a screaming man and a young woman lay sprawled on the sidewalk, blood oozing from their bullet-ridden bodies. As the barrage of bullets continued, she watched in horror as Cohen, holding his bloody shoulder, shouted commands. The bodyguard Cooper, shot in the stomach, was still gripping his revolver when Cohen and the other cop struggled to hoist him into the car. The wounded gangster quickly climbed into the back seat next to Cooper, staying low as the big bullet-proof Cadillac roared into the night.

Over the years Mickey Cohen had been bombed, shot, beat up, and imprisoned, but somehow miraculously managed to survive 11 attempts on his life from opposing gangsters. His luck however, ran out in 1950 when he was subpoenaed to testify about his suspected criminal activity during the Kefauver Hearings. As a result of this investigation Cohen was convicted of tax evasion and sentenced to four years at Alcatraz. Upon his release from prison, his life as a criminal appeared to end: he became a minor celebrity appearing as a guest on numerous television talk shows discussing his former gangster life.

In 1961, again Cohen was convicted of tax evasion and sent away to Alcatraz. While he was doing time on "The Rock" he survived another assault on his life when he fought off another inmate's attack with a lead pipe. When Alcatraz was closed down, Cohen was transferred to the Federal Penitentiary at Atlanta and released from there in 1972. Then as a free man, once more Cohen continued touring the U.S. doing radio and television talk shows.

Finally, after nearly 60 years of crime the Hollywood gangster who led a charmed and violent life died peacefully in his sleep of natural causes July 29, 1976. He was 62.

* * *

Chapter 7

MOE DALITZ: THE
GODFATHER OF LAS VEGAS

*P*erhaps no mobster in the history of America became more revered for his contributions to legitimate society than Moe Dalitz, known as the godfather of Las Vegas. In December 1899, Morris Barney Dalitz was born into a working class family in Boston. When he was still a young boy the family moved to Michigan, where his father opened the Varsity Laundry in Ann Arbor to serve University of Michigan students. Moe—as he was known to his friends—apparently inherited his entrepreneurial bent from his father. Barely into his twenties, it was during Prohibition Dalitz used his father's laundry trucks to smuggle booze from Detroit to Cleveland.

Already well known for his bootlegging and racketeering activities throughout the Midwest, the young opportunist ran roadside gambling joints from Michigan to Ohio and Kentucky. Passage of the Volstead Act on October 28, 1919, outlawing alcohol production and distribution, had handed Moe the business opportunity of a lifetime.

The millions that Dalitz reaped from his illegitimate enterprises he shrewdly invested in legitimate businesses in the Midwest and eventually in Las Vegas, providing himself with an aura of respectability. Unlike the Prohibition-era bootleggers who flocked to Las Vegas and continued to operate in the shadowy underworld, Dalitz shook off his early-won infamy and made an outward transition from Mafioso to philanthropist and legitimate citizen. His net worth mushroomed to over $100 million, which he shared with his associates, many of whom became millionaires as real estate developers.

EARLY MOB TIES

Moe Dalitz started out with the notorious Purple Gang in Detroit, but he also belonged to the equally nefarious Mayfield

Road Gang, according to law enforcement agencies in Cleveland. Years later during the 1951 Kefauver hearings, testimony from a Cleveland police officer identified Moe Dalitz as part of the gangster element that gave rise to organized crime in that Ohio city. "Ruthless beatings, unsolved murders and shakedowns, threats and bribery came to this community as a result of gangsters' rise to power," said the officer of Dalitz's early "business" methods.

By the 1930s, Dalitz had a very impressive list of legitimate businesses, holding ownership interest in a variety of companies: The Michigan Industrial Laundry in Detroit, Pioneer Linen Supply, Milco Sales, Dalitz Realty, Berdene Realty, and the Detroit Steel Company in Cleveland. Unlike ordinary peddlers of illicit rum and bathtub gin, who battled for territories on the Cleveland streets in so-called Whiskey Wars, Dalitz ferried Canadian whiskey in trucks floating on barges across Lake Erie. He developed a clever method of using a floating buoy to mark the contraband, all of which could be thrown overboard and sunk to the bottom if he encountered police. Then, after the authorities left the area, Dalitz could retrieve the contraband that had been marked by the buoy. While the common bootleggers of the Prohibition era wound up either dead or imprisoned, Dalitz came away unscathed.

With the repeal of Prohibition in 1933, Dalitz already had a string of illicit casinos operating, including the Pettibone Club, the Jungle Inn, the Mound Club, the Lookout House, and the Beverly Hills Club. He was also known to have a partnership with the Maceo Syndicate, which ran Galveston and supplied liquor from Canada and Mexico. Dalitz once joked to a friend, "How was I to know those gambling joints were illegal? There were so many judges and politicians in them I figured they had to be all right."

Dalitz was patriotic too, and served honorably in the U.S. Army during the early 1940s, earning the rank of captain. After the end of World War II, he found life at home in the Midwest difficult. America had changed since the so-called roaring twenties and early 1930s, when drinking alcohol and gambling in an underground speakeasy, though illegal, wasn't considered a social scourge. Postwar, nonetheless, all that changed. Law enforcement and high-ranking politicians cracked down hard on illegal gambling.

DALITZ BUYS INTO LAS VEGAS

By the late 1940s, Meyer Lansky, one of the lead architects of modern organized crime, had invested millions in Cuban casinos. To the Feds, Dalitz played an integral role inside Lansky's powerful organization, though he only dabbled in Cuban casinos. Dalitz was more impressed with Nevada's bright future, so he moved to Las Vegas, a vibrant city within the only state in the continental USA where gambling had been legalized. There he found his oasis, where gifted men with special gaming skills were respected and could thrive in a non-hostile environment. Moe's first business acquisition in Las Vegas, the still unfinished Desert Inn, opened in 1950. Wilbur Clark had begun building the resort, but much like Billy Wilkerson before him, Clark unfortunately ran out of money before completing construction. Dalitz led a group of financial backers from Cleveland, including Sam Tucker, Thomas McGinty, and Morris Kleinman, to fund the last phases of the resort's construction. When the Desert Inn finally opened, Clark was the designated front man and public face of the resort, while Dalitz remained in the background as the principal owner.

Within a year of the Desert Inn's opening, Dalitz was called to testify at the Kefauver Hearings, and more than held his own. In one exchange, Kefauver questioned Dalitz about the source of funding for Las Vegas investments: "...You did get yourself a pretty good little nest-egg out of rum running, didn't you?"

Dalitz replied, "Well, I didn't inherit any money, Senator... If you people wouldn't have drunk it, I wouldn't have bootlegged it."[68]

THE NEED FOR SELF-PRESERVATION

Like his long-time friend Meyer Lansky, the grand strategist who first moved the Mafia's money and power into Las Vegas, Moe Dalitz understood that volatile men were not accustomed to reasoning together; that in order to survive, a united front was needed. The best method to ensure cohesion among competing mob families was to blend. Thus, partnerships were formed when Mafia-made men married off their sons and daughters into rival clans in the cause of self-preservation.

Likewise, in Las Vegas, Dalitz became the chief arbiter for the men who owned Las Vegas. An interesting example of conflict resolution among The Mobster casino owners in Las Vegas occurred during construction of the Stardust (nee Starlite)—by far the largest resort of its day. Moe Dalitz feared the Stardust would provide too much competition. With the threat of a Mob war looming, Dalitz called for a meeting among the big casino operators, most of whom flew in from out of town, including

Dalitz's men Morris Kleinman and Longy Zwillman. Meyer Lansky chaired the meeting. The outcome was a negotiated settlement in which each of the owners received an interest in each other's hotels. As a bonus, lawyers arranged the agreement to prevent the government from knowing who owned what.

Later in his life, Moe Dalitz was responsible for building a championship golf course surrounded by multi-million dollar homes, with the picturesque Desert Inn at the forefront. According to a Dalitz protégé Irwin Molasky, "Moe was an innovative thinker." It was Moe's idea to give his hotel guests something extra—so he conceived building a golf course in the midst of mansion-like homes, all in the shadow of the beautiful Desert Inn. Moe was the innovator behind bringing the Tournament of Champions PGA Tour event to Las Vegas, giving the city a shot in the arm from beneficial publicity. By using Wilbur Clark's affable image and by inserting the necessary money into the project, Moe Dalitz created the classiest gaming palace in the budding casino-resort community.

After the death of Tony Cornero in 1955, Dalitz helped supervise completion of the Stardust Resort & Casino. Then, in 1958, funded by millions in Teamsters loans with additional backing from Louis Jacobs' Emprise Corp., Dalitz and his affiliates took over the Stardust from a crew led by Jake "The Barber" Factor. These skilled, experienced gamers converted the Stardust into a huge winner by expanding the hotel and gaming area, and introducing the Parisian-style floor show, the *Lido de Paris*. This change paved the way for many firsts in Las Vegas, including the first extravagant topless revue in a casino resort, and later the renowned illusionists Siegfried & Roy.

Dalitz ran the Desert Inn until 1967, when he sold it to billionaire tycoon Howard Hughes. That sale marked the beginning of Hughes's famous $300 million spending spree, which ultimately made him the biggest casino operator in Nevada. For Dalitz, the sale of the Desert Inn was an opportunity to get the authorities off his back. By this time a whole line of posh casino imitators had built lavish resorts along the Las Vegas Strip, including Caesars Palace, the Sands, the Dunes, Aladdin, and Tropicana. So-called Sin City was emerging from its Mob image, even though plenty of shady characters remained on the casino floor. Hughes, a novice casino operator when he purchased the Desert Inn, neglected to weed out the bandits stationed at craps table three. Though the table was listed as closed on the daily work sheet, the floor bosses and dealers reportedly spent months taking home the cash box and dividing it up!

DALITZ'S LATER YEARS

Long after the sale of the Desert Inn, Moe worked out of the Paradise Development office on Maryland Parkway, across the street from Sunrise Hospital, the medical facility he was largely responsible for financing and building.

Over the years critics came and went. Meanwhile, Dalitz continued amassing his financial empire and dutifully paying his taxes. He endured nearly a lifetime of criminal activity allegations, yet was indicted only twice—once in Buffalo in 1930, and once 35 years later in Los Angeles for tax evasion. Both charges were dismissed.

Dalitz shied away from interviews, which typically led back to his bootlegger days in the Midwest. Those who knew the man leading a secret life claimed, "he was not without a sense of humor and his own sense of image-making." Dalitz once told a local reporter for the *Las Vegas Review-Journal*, "When I left home it was during Prohibition in Ann Arbor, Michigan, and I went into the liquor business while it was illegal. Then when the repeal came along, we went into the casino business in Kentucky and Ohio, where it was illegal. I learned everything I know there."[69]

Over the years, Moe impressed Las Vegas business leaders with his business acumen and success. On the other hand, those who engaged in the evils of Las Vegas gambling, such as authors Ed Reid and Ovid Demaris, were less impressed, evidenced by their 1963 book, *The Green Felt Jungle*. Their conclusion—that "he was a little mobster from Cleveland,"—was similar to the opinion of law enforcement excerpted from a chapter criticizing Dalitz for his racketeering days and notorious ties to known mobsters. The authors wrote that Dalitz "was still a hoodlum in conscience and mind, but his heart has weakened."[70]

The seasoned Moe Dalitz was more complex than people realized. At a time when most gaming executives were busy serving their self interests, Dalitz found time to help other Las Vegans. His influence with Jimmy Hoffa, for example, secured Teamster loans for more than casinos. Even though his initial ties with the Teamster boss were less than friendly, Dalitz later showed he had clout with Hoffa by securing in 1959, a $1 million low-interest Teamster loan to build Sunrise Hospital.

Other examples of clout came in the form of loans to

construct a golf course and shopping malls at a time when most lending institutions shunned Las Vegas entrepreneurs. Marydean Martin, a Las Vegas advertising executive and friend of Dalitz, once said, "Moe was always such a gentleman. He gave back to the community. When the Maude Frazier Building (at UNLV) was built, it had no furniture. He bought all the furniture and didn't want anybody to know about it. He was that kind of person. Moe almost never complained, but he was feeling down. He said, 'I'll bet your grandpa drank whiskey,' and I said that he did. 'I'm the guy who made the whiskey, and I'm considered the bad guy. When does the time ever come that you're forgiven?' I said, 'I don't know.' It was one of the very few times he ever said anything about it."[71]

Dalitz regularly donated to the Las Vegas Public Library system as well as other community organizations. He took pride in helping performers such as Frank Sinatra get their first breaks in show business. During his later years, Moe Dalitz counted among his frequent visitors such well-known personalities as Senate Majority Leader Harry Reid, Barbara Walters, Frank Sinatra, Suzanne Somers, Wayne Newton, and Buddy Hackett.

Because Las Vegas was an "open city" in Mob Syndicate terms, no single crime family owned the city; it was open for business to all the crime families. With their early financing of the Desert Inn, the Cleveland Mob got an advanced foothold in the Las Vegas casino business, which gave Dalitz a head start in building his fortune. Despite his investments in legitimate businesses, his high-profile philanthropy, and his standing in Las Vegas society, the FBI believed—according to James Neff in his acclaimed *Mobbed Up*—that Moe Dalitz never relinquished his ties to The Mob.

By the late 1970s, a pillar of Las Vegas casino society, Dalitz became the subject of a *Penthouse* magazine article, "La Costa: The Hundred-Million-Dollar Resort with Criminal Clientele." The article reported on the development of a San Diego spa, Rancho La Costa, funded by the Teamsters. The article named names, characterizing the spa as in effect run by criminals for the pleasure of a criminal clientele. Moe Dalitz and his co-investors, including Irwin Molasky, Merv Adelson, and Allard Roen, filed a defamation suit. They lost initially, and later settled on repeal with a letter of clarification.

In 1976, Dalitz was named Humanitarian of the Year by the American Cancer Research Center and Hospital. Six years later he received the Torch of Liberty Award from the Anti-Defamation League of B'nai B'rith. Most notably, in 1979 he set up the Moe Dalitz Charitable Remainder Unitrust, a million-dollar fund to be divided upon his death. Because the last casino he built was the Sundance in downtown Las Vegas, later renamed the Fitzgerald, no fewer than 14 nonprofit organizations shared $1.3 million when he passed away at age 90. He is remembered as a philanthropist and tireless worker who helped mold Las Vegas into a modern city.

* * *

Chapter 8

JIMMY HOFFA—THE MAN BEHIND THE TEAMSTER LOANS THAT MADE LAS VEGAS

*a*rguably the most intriguing mystery in American history is what happened to Teamster President Jimmy Hoffa. Hoffa was last seen alive July 30,

1975, outside the Machus Red Fox restaurant in suburban Detroit. Hoffa's mysterious disappearance gave rise to a good deal of speculation about his whereabouts, one of which claims that his remains are buried under Giants Stadium, New Jersey, although no evidence has been found. Another rumor claims Hoffa's dead body was stuffed in a 55-gallon oil drum, compacted, and shipped to Japan as scrap metal. Others don't bother to speculate on the whereabouts of the body, including the FBI, yet most people theorize Hoffa was murdered by a contract killer, in part because of what he knew about The Mob in Las Vegas.

HOFFA'S EARLY LIFE

James Riddle "Jimmy" Hoffa was born February 14, 1913, and served with the International Brotherhood of Teamsters (IBT) union from 1932 to 1975. He played a key role in the development and growth of the union, which eventually became the largest union in America, with more than 1.5 members during his term as General President. From the mid 1950s through the mid 1970s, Jimmy Hoffa was the king of organized labor in America. His rapid climb from blue-collar origins within the IBT goes back to the early 1930s as a grocery worker, and later as a tough union organizer.

As Hoffa achieved greater prominence within the Teamsters, much of his elevated success was derived, in part, from friendships forged with upper echelon organized crime figures across the country. The Mob helped keep Hoffa in power. In return, through kickbacks and other unwritten benefits, Hoffa turned the Teamster's pension fund into The Mob's private bank.

Hoffa's association with Las Vegas began in 1959, when he appointed Mob-connected businessman Allen Dorfman to administer the pension fund through Valley Bank. One of the first gangsters to benefit from Teamster funds was the so-called godfather of Sin City Moe Dalitz, when that same year he arranged a $1 million Teamster loan to build Sunrise Hospital. Years later, it was discovered that Sunrise Hospital had been used covertly as a conduit for the casino skim. Ed Becker reported on a televised A & E story, "that someone would fly into Vegas, stay a few days at Sunrise then be sent off to Chicago or other suspicious Midwest locales wrapped in bandages from head to toe with the casino skim tucked underneath."[72]

THE HOFFA /DALITZ ALLIANCE

The account of the relationship between Jimmy Hoffa and Moe Dalitz has its origins in 1949, during the early years of union organizing in Detroit. Dalitz owned the Michigan Industrial Laundry, and an interesting conflict developed between the two when the future Teamster president tried to unionize Dalitz's laundry workers. The Detroit Teamsters local demanded a five-day work week for laundry drivers, and Dalitz responded by hiring Mafia enforcers to head off the union organizers.

Author Dennis Griffin wrote, "Laundry owners, including Dalitz, strongly opposed the union's position. Negotiations reached an impasse, with each side unwilling to budge. Dalitz, the shrewd businessman, saw a way around the issue. He had the owner representatives bypass the local's negotiator, Isaac Litwak, and reach out directly to its former business agent and current leader of the Detroit Teamsters, Jimmy Hoffa. Agents of the laundry owners asked what it would take for Hoffa to intervene on behalf of the owners. Hoffa's man said $25,000 would do the trick. The owners agreed. Neither side bothered to inform Litwak of the developments." [73]

Griffin continued, "During a subsequent bargaining session, Litwak was confident he had the owners on the ropes. Late in that meeting the door opened and in walked Jimmy Hoffa. He told the group there would be no strike and he wanted the contract signed on the owners' terms, with no five-day work-week provision. The stunned Litwak had no choice but to comply."[74]

These events—the confrontation between Hoffa and Dalitz, and eventual payoff—seemed of no consequence at the time. Yet it spawned a strong financial relationship which grew into something phenomenal ten years later: millions in loans from the Teamster's Central State Pension Fund to finance The Mob-run casinos of Las Vegas. Dalitz ultimately would receive several multi-million Teamster loans to expand his casinos including the Desert Inn and Stardust, and to build a golf course and Boulevard Mall. Later, more pension fund millions financed Jay Sarno's Caesars Palace, Circus-Circus and many other casino resorts along the expanding Las Vegas Strip.

Before Jimmy Hoffa opened coffers to the Teamster pension fund, Nevada's casino developers lacked the financial resources in the 1950s available to them today. In those days banks refused to lend money to the nefarious entrepreneurs building Las Vegas casinos. These were the days before the likes of billionaire Howard Hughes started buying up Nevada casinos like they were children's toys, before Wall Street and corporate

America solicited the public to purchase gaming stock, and before Michael Milken created junk-bond financing, which in 1989 financed Steve Wynn's construction of the Mirage. Before these sources became available, the only viable source of casino financing was The Mob with their suitcases full of illicit cash.

HOFFA IN PRISON

In 1964, Jimmy Hoffa was convicted of jury tampering, attempted bribery, and fraud. After exhausting the appeal process, Hoffa was sentenced in 1967 to a term of 13 years at Lewisburg Federal Prison in central Pennsylvania. In 1971, after serving almost five years of his sentence, Hoffa resigned the Teamster's presidency, an action that was part of a pardon agreement with President Richard Nixon. Hoffa was released from prison later that same year, although Nixon prohibited him from union activities until 1980.

In his 2004 book, "*I Heard You Paint Houses*," author Charles Brandt documents a taped confession with Frank Sheerhan, who had been a fellow union leader and close friend to Jimmy Hoffa. According to Sheerhan the pardon was executed after Hoffa arranged a $500,000 "political donation" to Nixon's re-election campaign, cash that was hand delivered to Nixon's Attorney General John Mitchell by none other than Frank Sheerhan. Unbeknownst to Hoffa, though, the pardon came with a significant string attached—Hoffa was not allowed any involvement whatsoever in union functions until 1980, the date his 13-year prison term expired, had he served the full sentence.

But the always belligerent Hoffa had never agreed to such a stipulation—the years in prison were spent planning his return to presidency of the Teamsters, and nothing was going to get in his way. Hoffa fought to overturn the order blocking him from union activity and tried to regain Teamster support. There was another stumbling block too, for the ex-union leader—the hand-picked Frank Fitzsimmons was the successor to the union presidency and was not willing to step down for Hoffa.

While Hoffa was doing time in prison, The Mob discovered they preferred doing business with the more pliable Fitzsimmons, instead of Hoffa. The even-tempered Fitzsimmons could easily be controlled by The Mob, while the pugnacious Hoffa could not. This was only one reason The Mob preferred Hoffa out of the picture. Fitzsimmons had an aura of respectability about him which was a perfect cover for the corruption lurking beneath the Teamsters. He was also a friend of Nixon and often a guest at the White House. Hoffa, on the other hand, was a tough ex-con, not the ideal image for the Teamster presidency.

The Mob was also concerned that Hoffa, after his release from prison, might reveal the connection between Teamster loans to Mob-run Las Vegas casinos, and the millions in skimmed money being removed from casino count rooms. Thus, Hoffa had to go!

HOFFA'S KILLER REVEALED

In his acclaimed book, "*I Heard You Paint Houses,*" former prosecutor and author Charles Brandt doesn't speculate about what happened to Jimmy Hoffa—because he claims to know who did it and what happened to Hoffa's corpse. Brandt said he knows who Hoffa's killer is because he did a deathbed interview with the triggerman who told him why Hoffa had to go, and admitted to the killing.

Not unlike others who are curious about Hoffa's disappearance, author Charles Brandt, too, is fascinated about what happened that fateful day in 1975. But unlike the masses who listen to idle speculation and whispered rumors, Brandt says the assassin's name is Hoffa's trusted friend and former Teamster official Frank Sheerhan, and he admitted to the killing while dying of cancer as detailed in Brandt's book.

Brandt wrote, "In 1967, Jimmy Hoffa had become president of the Teamsters and he needed some muscle. He contacted Mob boss Russell Bufalino, who was one of his closest underworld allies, looking for muscle. Russell put Sheerhan on the phone, and the first words on the phone, and the first words that Hoffa uttered to Sheerhan were 'I heard you paint houses,' and that means you kill people. The paint is the blood that spatters on the floor. And Sheerhan said, 'I do my own carpentry work too.' That means you dispose of the bodies."

Frank the Irishman Sheerhan, a huge man who stood 6'4"and weighed 250 pounds, allegedly murdered 24 people most of them fellow gangsters, including the ordered hit of New York Mafia don Crazy Joe Gallo. Sheerhan worked for Bufalino, who told Sheerhan to go to work for Hoffa. Sheerhan became his East Coast guy when Hoffa needed someone to handle rebellious members or opposing unions muscling in on Teamster turf. In return, Hoffa created a Teamsters local in Delaware and put Sheerhan in charge. Hoffa and Sheerhan became very close. He often traveled with Hoffa. After Hoffa went to prison, Sheerhan regularly visited him. Nevertheless, The Mob hired Sheerhan to do the hit on Hoffa.

Sheerhan remarked in the Brandt interview, "When it's time for you to go, they'll send your best friend. You'll be talking about a football bet, and the next thing you know, you'll be dead. And they selected Sheerhan to kill Hoffa because at the time Hoffa was very leery. He knew he had enemies that wanted him dead." [75]

THE MEETING IN DETROIT

In early 1975 Hoffa came to Las Vegas to meet with Moe Dalitz and the Detroit mobster "Tony Jack" Jacalone. The purpose of the meeting was to work out the differences between Hoffa and Anthony "Tony Pro" Provenzano, known as a made man with the Genovesse crime family of New Jersey. The one-time friends, Hoffa and Provenzano, had become bitter enemies after serving together at Lewisburg Prison. As the story goes, Provenzano wanted to build a restaurant with Teamster funds, and Hoffa was unable to arrange the funding. A fist fight between the two men ensued and Provenzano threatened to kill Hoffa's children. In time, Moe Dalitz was asked to be the arbiter between Hoffa and Provenzano.

After the meeting in Las Vegas, Hoffa agreed to a meeting in Detroit with his nemesis Tony Provenzano, to work out their differences. There was one condition, though: Hoffa insisted that his trusted friend Frank Sheerhan be at his side for the meeting in Detroit. But according to Sheerhan, in the 2003 interview with Brandt, even though Sheerhan was a personal friend of Hoffa, The Mob ordered him to do the hit. Sheerhan said, "You don't say no or you will be dead. It was a matter of carrying out the hit or be killed myself."[76]

Sheerhan went on to say that, "He was one of three men to pick up Hoffa that day. He told Hoffa the meeting had been moved to a house a short distance from the restaurant on Beaverland Street. So Hoffa got into the back seat."

Arriving at the house, Hoffa walked in with Sheerhan behind him. Soon after they entered Sheerhan put two bullets in the back of Jimmy's head. The body was bagged and taken to an incinerator at a nearby funeral parlor. The whole thing was over in less than an hour, and by 6pm that evening Hoffa's remains were in ashes. The other two men already at the house, Tom and Steve Andretta, were the "cleaners." They cleaned up the blood and removed Hoffa's body. Steve Andretta died a few years ago, but Tom still lives in Las Vegas.

Years later, investigators did find traces of blood in the Detroit house where Sheerhan confessed he killed Hoffa in, but unfortunately they determined the blood was too old for conclusive testing.

Near the end of Sheerhan's life, lying on his deathbed with inoperable cancer, he made a confession to Brandt on tape.

"There is no question Frank Sheerhan was telling me the truth," Brandt said.

Stan Hunterton, a retired strike force prosecutor of organized crime said, "It got the town started, before banks would loan money, that's where you got money to start building casinos." [77]

Author Charles Brandt thinks Las Vegas should build a statue of Jimmy Hoffa. Brandt believes the growth of the Strip would never have happened without funding from the Teamster pension fund. Brandt, of course, was aware that Hoffa was no angel and that the union president was knee-deep in consorting with Mafia dons. Every one of those Teamster loans came with strings attached, such as kickbacks and stipulations that allowed The Mob to install its own key employees who skimmed millions from casino cash boxes.

Jimmy Hoffa was declared legally dead November 30, 1982, precisely seven years after he vanished in suburban Detroit. To date, no one has ever been convicted in the murder of Jimmy Hoffa. At the time of his disappearance he was 62.

* * *

Chapter 9

ANTHONY "JOE BATTERS" ACCARDO

Considered by law enforcement as one of the most dangerous and clever American gangsters of his era, Tony Accardo made his bones in the Chicago gang wars of Alphonse Capone and Elliot Ness. It was during Prohibition that Accardo earned the "Joe Batters" nickname from Capone himself, due to his skill at battering a pair of mob traitors with a baseball bat at a dinner Capone held just to kill the two men. Chicago newspapers later dubbed Accardo "Big Tuna" after he reportedly caught a giant tuna during a deep sea fishing excursion. After his rise to power within the Capone Mob, the FBI often referred to him as the "genuine godfather," while his friends and those that knew him well simply called him "Joe."

As the bodies piled up, Capone's youngest lieutenant schemed and murdered his way to the top of the Chicago Mob's hierarchy. It was during Accardo's tenure as overlord that the Chicago Mob experienced its greatest rise to wealth and power, expanding into new operations and territories. At the pinnacle of his criminal career, Accardo owned points in many of Las Vegas' prime resorts, including the Tropicana, Riviera, Stardust, and the Sands.

EARLY LIFE

Born Anthony Leonado Accardo of Sicilian immigrants on April 28, 1906, he grew up in the poor neighborhoods of Chicago's West Side. To help make money for his struggling family, at age 14 Accardo, with parental approval, dropped out of school and began cutting his teeth as a young tough with the Circus Café Gang, one of several juvenile street gangs which served as future talent pools for the city's adult criminal organizations.

In 1926, Accardo was befriended and recruited by Jack "Machine Gun" McGurn, one of Alphonse Capone's toughest hit men and reputed architect of the infamous St. Valentine's Day Massacre. As a soldier Accardo rose from small-time thug to one of Capone's many bodyguards. Accardo would prove himself on September 20, 1926, when a parade of 11 cars occupied by rival

North Side Gang assassins, armed with machine guns, attacked Capone's Cicero headquarters, the Hawthorne Inn. Thousands of rounds tore into the building, but the moment the bullets began flying the alert Accardo pulled Capone to the floor and lay on top of him to protect his boss from the ambush. When the assault was over only a few bystanders had been wounded, but incredibly no one was killed. Accardo's bravado that day earned him a position as one of Capone's top protectors, and in time he was given more important assignments.

Al Capone was sent to prison in 1931 to serve an 11-year term for tax evasion: his successor was Frank "The Enforcer" Nitti. About this time Accardo was rising as a top earner, loan sharking and distributing untaxed alcohol and cigarettes, so Nitti gave him more responsibility allowing him to establish his own crew: he was also named as the mob's head of enforcement. Accardo was now making a lot of money and on his way to becoming an established top wise guy. Not unlike all capo regimes that thrived in the underworld, Accardo received from his crew members five percent of their earnings as a so-called "street tax." In return, Accardo paid a tax to the family boss.

As the 1940s unfolded, it became evident that several top Chicago mob bosses, including Frank Nitti, would be indicted for their roles extorting unions in the Hollywood movie industry. However, Nitti was claustrophobic, and thus he feared being incarcerated in a jail cell serving a second term (the first for tax evasion). For that reason, to avoid prison, "upon his indictment in 1943, Nitti went out onto the Illinois Central Railroad track near his west suburban home and shot himself in the head with his

.38."[78] Nitti's underboss, Paul Ricca replaced him as top boss and named Accardo as underboss. Together, Ricca and Accardo ruled the Chicago mob for the next 30 years.

THE OUTFIT

Commencing in June 1960, for more than 20 years important clandestine meetings were convened every Thursday night in the fashionable River Forest suburb of Chicago at 915 Franklin Avenue, the mansion of Joe Accardo. The participants were Accardo's lifelong friend Murray Humphries, along with Paul Ricca and one other unknown man. These four men were part of a hierarchy: the heirs apparent to the notorious criminal organization once lead by "Scarface" Al Capone. Notably, it was Capone's downfall in 1931 that provided a fundamental lesson for the Accardo-Ricca generation: "exaggerated violence and a high media profile were the kiss of death and were to be avoided at all costs. Hundreds of millions were at stake, an amount not worth gambling for the luxury of being seen with movie stars. That was for amateurs."[79] The participants at these covert weekly conferences prided themselves by being effectively invisible while conducting their nefarious business affairs. "We don't want to be an item on television's nightly news, or it's all over," one was heard to say. This phrase became a moral standard for its wisest members. Law enforcement was, of course, aware of this criminal organization, yet because it was so cloaked and run so efficiently that proof of its existence was difficult to gather—especially during its first 50 years or so.

This new hierarchy of "invisible" Chicago gangsters was not "La Cosa Nostra" as described by Joe Valachi when he sang for the Feds in front of McClellan's Committee in 1963. Nor was it the syndicate of East Coast mobsters called "The Mafia," known for its Moustache Petes that performed ritualistic customs and fought notorious wars between ruling crime families during Prohibition. This band of brothers was different; they had cast off the more objectionable traits of Capone's mob that caused such mayhem during Prohibition. Instead, this new regime of progressive capos that came to reign over Chicago's criminal activities "shared as much commonality with Capone as modern-day man does with Cro-Magnon cave dwellers. Perhaps as a nod to their enlightened, modernized dominion a new name quickly emerged for the Chicago crime organization: The Outfit."[80]

During this progressive Accardo era, The Outfit expanded into supplying slot machines into gas stations, restaurants, and bars throughout its territory. Accardo also put The Outfit in Havana casinos in joint ventures with the New York crime families who had bribed Batista, the president of Cuba at the time, to allow gambling there. In Las Vegas, Accardo made sure every Mob-run casino used his slot machines. In Oklahoma and Kansas, Accardo took advantage of state laws prohibiting alcohol sales to introduce bootlegged alcohol. In doing so, The Outfit eventually dominated organized crime throughout most of the Midwest and Western U.S.

Accardo was the brains behind minimizing The Outfit's exposure to legal prosecution by phasing out certain traditional Mafia activities, such as extortion and labor racketeering. Another Accardo brain child was conversion of The Outfit's brothel business into call girl services, which made it more difficult for law enforcement to bust criminal activity by eliminating a vulnerable place of business. The result of these innovations proved very profitable for the Chicago boys, with greater influence, and less risk for Outfit members. By maintaining a low profile, and allowing the more dapper, outgoing bosses like Sam Giancana to be in the spotlight, both men—Tony Accardo and Paul Ricca—who shared the top boss position—were able to run The Outfit longer than anyone, including Al Capone. Ricca once said, "Accardo had more brains for breakfast than Capone had in a lifetime."

ACCARDO AND THE RIVIERA

Another episode of Accardo's strong-arm techniques came about in an incident at the Riviera Hotel & Casino which opened in 1955. Soon after its opening, it was discovered that the casino had lost money consistently for 90 consecutive days. Accardo, the Riviera's de facto owner, knew that if a casino loses money every day over an extended period it had to be more than bad luck. Accardo immediately notified the official on-site owners—three brothers from Miami, David, Meyer, and Lou Gensberg—that they had 15 minutes to vacate the Riviera, or else! Aware of Accardo's ruthless reputation they, of course, left!

Accardo then "asked" Gus Greenbaum, a retired resort manager extraordinaire who had brought profitability to the fledgling Flamingo after Ben Siegel's demise, who was living in Phoenix, to come and save the Riviera. The problem was that Greenbaum enjoyed being retired and respectively declined Accordo's offer. As a consequence, three days later Greenbaum's sister-in-law was found murdered in her bed. Greenbaum, of course, got the message and reluctantly came to work for Accardo to cure the Riviera's financial ills.

By the time Greenbaum moved into one of the Riviera's owner's penthouse suites, the casino was in dire straits. It was virtually on the brink of bankruptcy, all caused by the Gensberg brothers who had just been thrown out. Author Steve Fischer writes, "Liquor had been disappearing from the storerooms, which found its way into the owners' suites, and personal items like cars were being paid for through the Riviera bank accounts. Plus, the Miami group of owners were gambling big every night at the Riviera's casino, losing thousands of dollars and then tearing up the markers!"[81] Even worse, the brothers had been taking turns skimming from the casino count room. Fischer added that, "In 1955 there was a practice among casino owners called 'Filling the Journal.'" Early casino owners liked to hang out in the soft count room, because that's where the money was. "The money in there was their money—they won it fair and square! So, if an owner walked into the soft count room with a thin *Las Vegas Review-Journal* under his arm, "and he came out with a BIG FAT *Review-Journal* folded under his arm, who was going to stop him?"[82] Eventually, the word got back to Accardo that there were too many Riviera owners "filling their journals."

By 1958, Gus Greenbaum, the shrewd accountant who over the years grew into a reputable resort manager for The Outfit, somehow had changed his ways. Soon after he became the Riviera's general manager, his excessive gambling, womanizing, and drug use turned to embezzling from casino cash boxes. It wouldn't be long before the Chicago bosses learned of Greenbaum's stealing. The end result occurred on December 3,

1958—a maid found Gus Greenbaum and his wife, Bess, dead in their Arizona home; their throats slashed Mafia style.

Meanwhile, by the late 1950s Accardo's opulent lifestyle instigated an IRS investigation that forced him to relinquish his position as The Outfit's top boss. He had enough power and all the money he needed, so he wisely stepped down for the next ten years, stayed out of the limelight, and officially claimed he worked as a beer salesman for a local brewery; unofficially Accardo remained an Outfit consigliere. He recommended that a young man who had made his bones and accomplished some fine things for The Outfit be appointed his successor. He was, and in 1957 the new leader of The Outfit became Sam Giancana.

According to FBI reports, by the late 1950s The Mob was skimming an estimated aggregate of $1 million a day from their Vegas casinos. During this period, Tony Accardo called for a meeting among the hidden owners of Mob-run Vegas casinos. The meeting's primary agenda—select a so-called "point man" to oversee and protect The Outfit's casino interests in Vegas. At the meeting Accardo suggested that there should be only one outside man, and it would be his responsibility to enforce The Outfit's policies in Vegas and oversee the casino skim: to protect it and to make sure the designated investors received their appropriate share.

The first to be assigned as the Vegas point man was Johnny Rosselli. Over the years he had served as underboss to Frank Nitti, Paul Ricca, and Tony Accardo. Rosselli, who proved more adept as emissary and negotiator, was quickly replaced by Marshall Caifano. He would oversee The Outfit's unreported profits skimmed from casino count rooms until 1971, when

Anthony Spilotro replaced Caifano. Paul Ricca died in 1972, leaving Accardo as the sole unofficial leader of The Chicago Outfit, although Joey Aiuppa fronted for him.

Remarkably, Accardo's invisibility was his strength, and what kept from ever spending a day in jail, despite damaging evidence against him and his lifelong association with organized crime. Joe Accardo died in Chicago on May 22, 1992 of congestive heart failure. He was 86.

* * *

Chapter 10

SAM "MOMO" GIANCANA

Salvatore "Momo" Giancana was a short, balding man who smoked Cuban cigars and talked out of the side of his mouth. He had a sixth grade education, drove a pink Cadillac, and was known to have at least 14 aliases—primarily Sam Flood, Momo Salvatore Giancana, and Moe or Mooney Giancana. Often, especially when he needed reservations, or traveled with celebrities, he introduced himself as Dr. Goldberg, or Mr. Morris. Frank Sinatra, his lifelong friend and those that knew him well, called him Sam.

Much like his unofficial overseer Joe Accardo, Sam Giancana owned points in the Tropicana, Riviera, Stardust, and Sands which brought him hundreds of thousands of dollars in skimmed money. He also had Outfit business interests in Miami Beach, St. Louis, Arizona, California, and Mexico, along with casinos in the Middle East and in Central America. The total annual take from these enterprises was estimated at $2 billion, of which $50 million went directly to Giancana. After Giancana was appointed lead boss of The Chicago Outfit he conducted most of his business at the Armory Lounge in Forest Park, Illinois. Away from the Armory Lounge, he held business meetings on the golf course or in a hearse, to keep the Feds from eavesdropping.

By 1960, Giancana had allegedly ordered the killing of at least two hundred men. Many of the victims were hung on meat hooks and tortured with ice picks and electric cattle prods, while some of them were simply shot.

A pint-sized dapper dresser, Sam Giancana wore sharkskin suits, alligator shoes and a star sapphire pinky ring given to him by Frank Sinatra. When Giancana knew the Feds were watching him, he added a black fedora and dark wraparound sunglasses. Above all else, from 1957 to 1966 Sam Giancana was known as Chicago Outfit's official top boss. Anything that involved loan sharking, prostitution, illegal gambling, narcotics, and extortion in the Chicago area, Sam Giancana got a piece of it.

EARLY LIFE

According to FBI files dated February 14, 1960, Giancana began his criminal career in Chicago joining the 42 Gang, a tough juvenile street crew answering to political boss Joseph Esposito. Giancana soon developed a reputation for being an excellent getaway driver, strong earner, and a vicious killer. He was arrested for murder in 1925, but when the prosecution's star witness, a cab driver named Alexander Burba, was found dead, with no witness to testify the charges against Giancana were dropped. After Esposito's murder, the fact that Giancana was a great "wheel man" with a getaway car and had a knack for making money on the street, he was recruited into the Capone mob in the late 1930s.

FBI files also noted that Giancana had been arrested 70 times for various crimes, including murder on three occasions, and spent much of the 1920s and 1930s in prison. Though never proven, it's most noteworthy that Chicago police suspected Giancana to be a driver and gunman in the St. Valentine's Day Massacre February 14, 1929, which killed seven rival Northside Gang members, though to date no one has ever been charged in the notorious slaughter.

In 1942, Giancana allegedly forced jazz musician Tommy Dorsey—by making him an offer he couldn't refuse—into releasing crooner Frank Sinatra out of his contract early, freeing Sinatra to pursue a solo career.

Out of prison, Giancana maintained close ties with Joe Accardo and by the early 1950s had risen to prominence within The Chicago Outfit. When Accordo stepped down as head boss in 1957, Giancana replaced him in day-to-day duties as The Outfit's top boss in name only; behind the scenes Accardo and Ricca sanctioned The Outfit's major decisions. This working relationship, however, would eventually fail. Unlike the inconspicuous Accardo who had a reputation as a happily married family man, Giancana lived an ostentatious lifestyle, frequently seen in public with different girlfriends and partying in posh nightclubs.

There were other problems, too. Many of The Outfit's upper echelon were unhappy when Giancana failed to distribute some of the lavish profits to the rank and file members from Outfit casinos in the Middle East and Central America. The same made members also believed that Giancana was attracting too much attention from the watchful eyes of the FBI, who everyone knew was following his pink Cadillac throughout the greater Chicago area.

REPUTED CIA CONNECTIONS

During the Kennedy administration, it was alleged that the Central Intelligence Agency (CIA) recruited Giancana and other gangsters to assassinate Cuban president Fidel Castro. The CIA reasoned that The Mob wanted revenge on Castro because after Batista's downfall he nationalized all Mob-run casinos in Havana, costing The Mob millions in lost property and revenue. This connection between JFK and Giancana is indicated in the "Exner File" authored by Judith Campbell Exner. "She allegedly was the mistress to both JFK and Giancana and claimed she was the link between the two delivering communications regarding Fidel Castro."[83]

By the mid 1960s, the FBI had suspicions that Frank Sinatra fronted for Giancana as a hidden owner when Sinatra purchased the Cal-Neva Lodge in Lake Tahoe, Nevada. Sam Giancana was listed in the Nevada Black Book, which by law prohibited him from stepping foot on the premises of a Nevada casino. During undercover surveillance, the FBI proved their allegation when they spotted Giancana at the Cal-Neva during a seven-day stay as a guest of Sinatra.

Unlike The Outfit's other top leaders—Joe Accardo and Paul Ricca in particular—who discreetly maintained a low profile and tried to stay out of the limelight, Giancana did the opposite. He seemed to relish in the public's attention and was frequently photographed with big-name celebrities like Sammy Davis Jr. and Dean Martin, who often performed at the Chicago night clubs Giancana owned. Over the years too, he had maintained a relationship with Phyllis McGuire, a member of the renowned trio of singers called the McGuire Sisters.

After Giancana was jailed in 1965 for contempt of court, he lost control as top man in The Outfit. Accardo and Ricca replaced him with Joey Aiuppa, and Giancana was exiled to Mexico. He remained in Mexico until the authorities arrested and deported him to the U.S. in June 1975. That same year, just a few days before he was subpoenaed to testify at Church Committee Hearings about his alleged conspiracy in a CIA plot to assassinate Fidel Castro, Sam Giancana was gunned down by an unknown assailant in the basement of his Chicago home. He was 67.

* * *

Chapter 11
THE MOB'S POINT MEN IN LAS VEGAS

*F*irst came the murder of the Flamingo's Bugsy Siegel; next was the slaying of the Riviera's sticky-fingered Gus Greenbaum along with two innocent family members. Apparently the dons back east who ruled the men of Las Vegas had problems finding the right man to look after their lucrative operations. Nevertheless, the boys had plenty of applicants interested in being overseers of Mob-controlled casinos. Among them was John Caifano from Chicago. His extensive police rap sheet included convictions for burglary, extortion, larceny, and interstate fraud. Together he and Frankie Carbo were suspects in Bugsy Siegel's murder, both having been in the Beverly Hills area that June night in 1947.

JOHN "MARSHALL" CAIFANO

Born Marchello Giuseppe Caifano in Sicily in 1911, he immigrated to New York City and later moved to Chicago, where he became a high-ranking member of the Chicago Outfit during Prohibition. Moving again to Las Vegas in 1951, Caifano changed his name to John Marshall when he was made overseer of Mob-controlled casinos. It was reported that in exchange for the "Don" chair of Las Vegas, Caifano's beautiful blond-haired wife, Darlene, was traded to Chicago boss Sam Giancana, a childhood pal of his. Caifano had been the go-to-guy for Chicago mobsters Joe Accardo and his underboss Sam Giancana.

Over the years Caifano became fascinated with car bombs, such as the one that blew Willie Bioff to bits and pieces November 1955 when The Outfit snitch turned the key to the ignition of his pickup truck. Nor was Caifano a novice at killing with a knife up close, a technique equally capable of sending a message to anyone who divulged too much information about Chicago wise guys. Years earlier, in 1943, Caifano was suspected in the torture and arson murder in Chicago of the speakeasy waitress Estelle Carey. The Outfit suspected Carey's boyfriend was cooperating in a police investigation, so she was ice-picked to death. To complete the message she was also set afire.

Johnny Tocco knew Caifano first-hand. A boxing trainer from St. Louis, Tocco moved to Las Vegas in the 1950s, having worked in the corners of the fight ring of many champions, including Sonny Liston. He described Caifano as one of the toughest characters he'd ever met: "Serious as a heart attack." Those were strong words coming from a corner man who worked in a world of tough professional fighters. About five-foot-five, Caifano was pure psychopath. A gray-eyed ex-boxer, he had a criminal record going back to childhood. When he moved to Chicago, he joined Giancana's 42 Gang as a debt collector. Rarely did he return empty handed. His penchant for violence defined his reputation, and he seemed to enjoy brutality. His sadistic nature was as effective as it was unnerving to those around him.

His arrival in Las Vegas as the new Mob enforcer didn't go unnoticed. Sheriff Ralph Lamb gave Caifano this option: "Keep a low profile, or get out of town." But like the tough Ben Siegel before him, Caifano loved the life of violence, money, and lust. He was also a psychopathic killer, like Siegel, and had no intention of keeping the fact that he had killed many people a secret. "We were all terrorized by this guy," said Ed Becker, an organized-crime expert and former Riviera publicist. "If he walked into your hotel, you made sure he got whatever he wanted. You never approached him. He always looked at you like he was looking for a gun in your hand. He was such an evil son of a bitch that you didn't dare cross his line. His attitude was, 'I'm a Mob guy. Don't fuck with me.'"[84] Those that did suffered.

BLAZE AT THE EL RANCHO

Caifano became a prime suspect in the mysterious fire that leveled the original El Rancho Vegas in June 1960, although charges were never filed. County arson investigators ruled the fire was accidental. Yet Ed Becker, a resident of a bungalow directly behind the El Rancho, recalled that Caifano had made several unsuccessful plays for the resort's chorus girls, earning his tough-guy routine and boorish behavior a boot from the property by the El Rancho owner, Beldon Katleman, mere hours before the fire. The police allegations only heightened Caifano's reputation as a scary psychopath not to be messed with.

Creation of the Gaming Control Board in 1955 and new gaming regulations had their first positive result when they brought about the fall of Caifano in Las Vegas. The psychopath had been arrested several times since 1930, yet it was the administrative process of posting him into the Nevada Black Book that led to his exclusion. (Nevada's Black Book, officially known as the List of Excluded Persons, is the state's list of notorious people so unsavory to legal gambling that they are prohibited from setting foot in a casino.) If he wasn't allowed inside the casinos, it would be difficult for him to communicate with or intimidate people.

Caifano qualified for the List of Excluded Persons not so much for his alleged brutal slaying of Estelle Carey but for his reputation, based on his being a suspect in a number of other murders. These included the unsolved killing of ex-Chicago police Lieutenant William Drury, the 1952 strangulation of gambler Louie Strauss, and the double-barreled shotgun murder of rackets insider Teddy Roe.

Ed Becker recalled seeing Caifano in the casinos during the 1950s, about the time the killer changed his name to Johnny Marshall. But even an alias couldn't disguise his sadistic nature, or the true reason he was in town: to shake down casino owners such as Beldon Katleman and Benny Binion on behalf of The Chicago Outfit.

By 1961, Caifano was added to the FBI's Ten Most Wanted List, and he decided to hide out at the Desert Inn, where he had friends. Unfortunately for him, after a few days of room service food, one of the staff reported Caifano's whereabouts, and the authorities put him in custody. The local news media got wind of Caifano's capture at the Desert Inn. When Caifano was escorted from the property, *Las Vegas Sun* photographer Frank Maggio was there on assignment. "Maggio approached Caifano, who took a swing at him, smashing his heavy Speed Graphic camera. Maggio reacted out of instinct, retaliating with a right cross that nailed Caifano flush on the chin, knocking him cold."[85]

Caifano's frightening career was far from over, however. As The Outfit's most productive torpedo, Caifano was suspected in another string of murders. These included the 1973 shotgun slaying of corrupt former Chicago chief investigator Richard Cain, and the 1977 car-bombing of oil millionaire Ray Ryan. Earlier, Ryan had testified in court that Caifano tried to extort $60,000 from him. Caifano ended up doing six years in prison for extortion. Unfortunately for Ryan, Caifano held a grudge against him, and two years after Caifano emerged from prison, Ryan's life brutally ended—Mafia style.

Caifano was finally put away for a long federal sentence in connection to the theft of 2,000 shares of unissued Westinghouse stock worth $2 million. He was sentenced in May 1980, to 20 years at the federal penitentiary in Sandstone, Minnesota. After an early release from prison incarcerated only 11 years, Caifano lived quietly in Fort Lauderdale, Florida. In stark contrast to the lifelines of Mob casino overseers Siegel and Greenbaum, doing time in prison seemed to extend Caifano's life expectancy; he died of natural causes in September 2003 at age 92.

"HANDSOME" JOHNNY ROSSELLI

Distinct from Caifano, the boorish tough guy with a hair-trigger temper, Johnny Rosselli was the dapper diplomat of The Chicago Outfit. Rosselli represented the boys' interests in both Hollywood and Las Vegas.

Born Filippo Sacco in Esperia, Italy, in July 1905, Rosselli immigrated to Boston in 1911, although at his later trial he testified under oath that he was born in Chicago. He had a checkered career. He fled to Chicago in 1922 after allegedly committing a murder, joined The Chicago Outfit, and changed his name to John Rosselli.

Rosselli moved to Los Angeles in 1924 and joined the Jack

155

Dragna crime family. After becoming friends with film producer Bryan Foy, the two of them produced several gangster movies. By 1940, Rosselli was involved in The Outfit's multi-million-dollar extortion campaign against the motion picture industry. In 1942, he joined the U.S. Army, and a year later was convicted of labor racketeering in the movie industry based on testimony of Willie Bioff. He served six years in prison. Upon his release, Rosselli became The Outfit's go-to guy and maintained his ties to the Dragna crime family.

From 1954 to 1957 Rosselli crisscrossed the country offering "juice" and protection in regions declared open territories by The Outfit, such as Las Vegas, where no single crime family controlled the city. "Juice" had two distinct meanings in Mafia lingo. For loan sharking, juice and vigorish (or the vig), were synonyms for the interest charged on a loan, but in gaming circles, the term referred to connections in the business. Rosselli extended his connections along the East Coast from Boston to Miami, and in the southwest from Arkansas to Vegas to L.A. Outside the country, he migrated to Cuba, where he was well known at Havana casinos, and to Guatemala, where he allegedly involved himself in 1950's politics and developed ties with the CIA.

ROSSELLI AND THE TROPICANA

In 1957, a consortium of mobsters led by Meyer Lansky, Carlos Marcello, and Frank Costello put together enough money to start construction on the Tropicana Hotel-Casino. Rosselli's role in Las Vegas began to take shape. He was assigned the responsibility of monitoring the project's expenses, for which he received a percentage of the lucrative gift shop concession.

Rosselli's police record and reputation for running with a rough crowd ultimately kept him from becoming a licensed casino owner. He realized, however, that his true calling was establishing high-end connections in legitimate American society. Rosselli went on to become known as the man who made the Tropicana successful. His skill in real estate development and finance was unmatched, as he helped facilitate loans through the Teamsters Central States Pension Fund. In addition, he was on site when the Riviera was built, and he filled its key executive positions with Chicago Outfit personnel.

When the Cuban Revolution ended in January 1959, Fidel Castro nationalized all The Mob's casinos in Cuba, closing them a year later. That put the mobsters out of business there costing them millions. It is no wonder that Rosselli, along with Outfit boss Sam Giancana and Tampa boss Santo Trafficante, became involved, via recruitment by the CIA, in the plot to kill the new Cuban dictator. Eleven years later, Rosselli became an intriguing subject in the Church Committee's investigation to resolve suspicions of conspiracy in the plot to kill President John F. Kennedy, as well as the failed attempt to assassinate Fidel Castro.

In 1963, Frank Sinatra sponsored Rosselli for membership in the exclusive Los Angeles Friars Club. Soon after his acceptance, Rosselli discovered an elaborate cheating scheme in a Friar's Club poker game run by one of his Las Vegas friends, Maury Friedman. Rosselli demanded a cut. Scores of wealthy men including actor Zeppo Marx and Harry Karl, husband of actress Debby Reynolds, were cheated out of millions of dollars.

About this time Las Vegas was beginning to lose its mobbed up image, especially with the emergence of Howard

Hughes. Yet, Johnny Rosselli was a Mob man and still had his hooks in unwanted places. He maintained a high profile, which some people thought too high. Finally, in December 1966, word got around to Clark County Sheriff Ralph Lamb that Rosselli was extorting money from some of the city's key casino licensees.

One particular evening in December of that same year, Sheriff Lamb learned Rosselli was in the coffee shop at the Desert Inn with its owner Moe Dalitz. Lamb sent in a rookie deputy with precise instructions: inform Mister Rosselli that the sheriff wanted to see him downtown.

"He told my guy to get lost, which he shouldn't have done," Sheriff Lamb recalled in a later interview. "I went in and helped him brush up on his manners."

What happened next was described by authors Charles Rappleye and Ed Becker: "Lamb strolled into the coffee shop, grabbed Rosselli by his silk necktie, lifted him out of the booth, then pulled him across the table and cuffed him about the head and shoulders all the way back to the patrol car. After handcuffs were snapped on, Lamb slammed Rosselli into the back seat."[86]

At the sheriff's office, Rosselli was thrown in a cage and hosed down with delousing agent like a flea-infested dog. From that mortifying moment on, Rosselli's star status dimmed, and his stature in Las Vegas diminished. Though his falling from grace didn't slow his criminal activity, his profile was slighted.

Just when things seemed bad for Rosselli, they got worse. In 1968, authorities discovered Rosselli never acquired lawful residency or citizenship in the United States, and he was tried and convicted of maintaining an illegal residence. The Immigration and Naturalization Service ordered him deported. However, Rosselli's

Italian homeland refused to accept him, so he remained in The United States. A year after his deportation hearings, authorities were about to get justice for his past criminal activity. The dapper Rosselli, renowned as a genius in the growth of gambling in Las Vegas and notorious as a key figure in the CIA plot to assassinate Fidel Castro, was suddenly convicted of rigging a poker game at the Friars Club in Los Angeles. In February 1969, he received a five year prison sentence. When released, Rosselli was a mere shadow of the well-connected man people once called Handsome Johnny. Nevertheless, he wasn't finished making headlines, which became a huge concern for the Mafia dons back east.

LATER LIFE

When Senator Frank Church's committee held hearings in Washington to discuss publicly, for the first time, several of the CIA's past undercover missions, Rosselli was subpoenaed to testify about the plot to kill Fidel Castro. Shortly before he was scheduled to appear, an unknown gunman shot and killed Sam Giancana. Giancana's murder alarmed Rosselli, whose own Mob influence vanished with Giancana's demise and impelled him to permanently leave Las Vegas for Florida.

During the hearings, the CIA and FBI agents who testified supported their testimony with files of notes. They also prepared working drafts to help them relate events. Rosselli had his own props, which seemed to impress Senator Barry Goldwater. Rosselli testified on June 24 and September 22 1975. The record shows the following exchange:

SENATOR GOLDWATER: Mr. Rosselli, it's remarkable to me how your testimony dovetails with theirs. Tell me, Mr.

Rosselli, during the time that all this was going on, were you taking notes?

WITNESS: Senator, in my business, we don't take notes.[87]

Throughout the hearings, Rosselli's testimony was reported as more colorful than informative. He kept his pledge of omertà, the Mafia code of silence, and never exposed his Mob associates. But the powers that be felt differently. When Rosselli returned to his home in Plantation, Florida, his boredom grew with each passing day. He refused to take seriously the warnings from his friends that his life was in danger.

John Rosselli was last seen alive on July 28, 1976. The following month his decomposing body was found in a 55-gallon oil drum floating in the bay near Miami. When the authorities discovered the drum they found Johnny Rosselli strangled and shot, his legs sawn off. It was believed that he gave public testimony without The Outfit's approval. Other theorists speculate that Castro paid him back for his participation in the failed plot to assassinate him.

In the absence of Rosselli, the boys back east, once again, began looking at potential candidates to oversee their casino interests in Las Vegas.

FRANK "LEFTY" ROSENTHAL

On October 4, 1982, Frank Rosenthal crossed the parking lot of the Marie Callendar's restaurant on East Sahara Avenue. The moment he keyed the ignition to his Cadillac it exploded in flame. A steel plate that reinforced the engine's firewall miraculously shielded Rosenthal from the blast, and he escaped with only minor injuries.

Before his car blew up, Frank Rosenthal was one of the most powerful and controversial men in Las Vegas. He was in charge of one of the largest casino operations in Las Vegas. Rosenthal gained notoriety as the man who brought sports betting to Las Vegas casinos—an achievement that made him famous in the chronicles of Sin City. Or, as Nicholas Pileggi wrote in his acclaimed book *Casino*, "He was a gamblers gambler, the man who set the odds, a perfectionist who had once astonished the kitchen help in the Stardust Hotel by insisting that every blueberry muffin had to have at least ten blueberries in it."[88]

EARLY YEARS

Born on Chicago's West Side in October 1929, Frank Rosenthal often skipped school so he could watch the Cubs play baseball. There, in the bleachers of Wrigley Field, he learned to

161

hone his skills at odds making and successful sports betting.

Rosenthal had been eluding trouble most of his life. Before going to work in legitimate casinos in 1971, Rosenthal started out in his late teens working for The Chicago Outfit as a clerk and a bookie. In fact, he had held only one legitimate job his whole life—he served from 1956 until 1958 as a military policeman in Korea.

In 1961, Rosenthal appeared before a congressional committee in Washington that was investigating organized crime in gambling.

By 1961 Rosenthal was living in Miami, Florida, as a nationally recognized professional sports handicapper and bettor. Often, he was reportedly seen there in the company of notorious Chicago Outfit members Jackie Cerone and Flore Buccieri. About this time Rosenthal was accused of match fixing and subpoenaed to appear before Senator McClellan's subcommittee on Gambling and Organized Crime. During the hearings Rosenthal would take the Fifth Amendment 37 times and wouldn't even reveal how he got his nickname "lefty" which, in fact, he earned as a kid for being left-handed.

As a result of the hearings Rosenthal was barred from all racing establishments in Florida, though he was never charged. "Despite his frequent arrests for illegal gambling and bookmaking, Rosenthal was convicted only once, pleading no contest in 1963, for allegedly bribing New York University point guard Ray Paprocky to shave points for a college basketball game in North Carolina. To escape police attention Rosenthal moved to Las Vegas in the late 1960s."[89]

Rosenthal's skill as an expert odds maker catapulted his reputation. He was given the responsibility of secretly running several Mob-controlled casinos, including the Stardust, Marina, Fremont, and Hacienda. Later, he pioneered the first Nevada sports book to operate within a casino, and developed the Stardust into the world's leading venue for sports betting.

Those in the know believed Rosenthal was one of a handful of men who set the odds for thousands of bookmakers from coast to coast. In addition, Rosenthal became known as the first employer in Las Vegas to hire female croupiers; the innovative move proved very profitable. Within a year income nearly doubled at the Stardust, and soon other Strip casinos followed suit in their hiring policy.

GAMING COMMISSION HEARING

In 1976, Nevada gaming authorities learned that Rosenthal was covertly operating casinos in Las Vegas without a gaming license. The Nevada Gaming Commission held a hearing to judge the feasibility of his obtaining a license. But Rosenthal was denied a license based on his nefarious associations with known mobsters, in particular his boyhood friendship with the notorious Chicago hood Anthony Spilotro.

Unable to obtain a necessary gaming license, Rosenthal designated himself Stardust's "Entertainment Director" and starred in a talk show publicizing the Stardust Casino. Originally televised from a studio, the show was moved to the casino sports book where Rosenthal's first guest was none other than Frank Sinatra, in his first ever talk-show appearance.

LATER YEARS

Due to his alleged ties to organized crime, in 1988 Rosenthal was entered into Nevada's Black Book. From then on, he was prohibited from entering Nevada casinos. He returned to Miami Beach, where he worked as a consultant and operated an offshore betting website. Frank Rosenthal died of heart failure in October 2008 in his Miami Beach home at age 79.

Frank Rosenthal was immortalized in the Nicholas Pileggi book *Casino*. His career as a Mob front man became further inspiration for the acclaimed 1995 Martin Scorcese film *Casino*, a fictionalized adaptation of Pileggi's true crime account. Rosenthal—re-named in the film Sam "Ace" Rothstein, was portrayed by Robert De Niro, and his long-time friend and Vegas enforcer Anthony Spilotro—re-named Nicky Santoro—was played by Joe Pesci.

ANTHONY SPILOTRO: THE VEGAS ENFORCER

Behind famed odds-maker *Frank Rosenthal was his boyhood friend, future overseer of the casino skim, and Vegas point man Anthony Spilotro. By the time of his murder in 1986, Anthony Spilotro, the five-foot five little tough guy from Chicago, was suspected by the Feds of at least 25 murders, not to mention the mayhem he caused during his sordid stay in Las Vegas. Spilotro was well-known to the FBI agent investigating organized crime in Las Vegas during the 1970s and 1980s, William F. Roemer Jr. In his biography of Spilotro, *The Enforcer*, the Bureau's most decorated agent told of the FBI's bugging the offices of the casinos, concentrating on those with known Mob ties. Even the FBI was surprised at the amount of cash skimmed and sent off to Chicago. Some estimates placed the combined amount at $1 million daily, in 1980's dollars.

SPILOTRO'S EARLY YEARS

Born Anthony John Spilotro in May 1938, the man known as the "enforcer" lived most of his life the way he died—brutally violent! Agent Roemer described the pint-sized Chicago hoodlum as ruthless, scheming, and as anti-social as any up and-coming gangster could be. Just a kid out of Steinmetz High, he exhibited a flair for extreme violence in the way he extorted lunch money from his classmates.

Spilotro dropped out of school in his sophomore year and became known for a string of petty crimes, such as purse snatching and shoplifting. His first arrest occurred in 1955. Before Spilotro hooked up with organized crime, he was arrested 13 times. In 1962 he was befriended by The Outfit's enforcer "Mad" Sam DeStefano, a notorious loan shark and one of the worst torture killers in the annals of crime in a city long recognized for violent inventiveness. Under the tutelage of DeStefano, Anthony Spilotro started out with The Chicago Outfit as a debt collector and rapidly became occupied in higher levels of criminal activity. DeStefano's preferred torture device was the ice pick. He exhibited his skills with painful impunity to his youthful pupil— Tony Spilotro—a recent high school dropout who seemed to relish the agony of others.

HE "MADE HIS BONES"

In 1962, Spilotro would "make his bones," to commit an ordered murder for the first time, in the notorious killings of

Jimmy Miraglia and Bill McCarthy. Spilotro was given orders to wipe out two young thieves who had robbed and shot three people in the mobster-populated neighborhood of Elmwood Park, near Chicago—an area designated off limits to any criminal activity by The Outfit. The two thieves were also reportedly in debt to Spilotro's old boss, Sam DeStefano. Spilotro found one of the young thieves, Bill McCarthy, clamped his head into an industrial vise, and squeezed it until he got McCarthy's confession to the whereabouts of his accomplice, Jimmy Miraglia.

Witnesses later reported that during the torture, McCarthy's eye popped out of its socket before he finally confessed. This head-in-the-vice method was vividly portrayed in Martin Scorcese's film *Casino* by the character Tony Dogs as the victim, and Nicky Santoro as Spilotro.

On May 15, 1962, McCarthy and Miraglia were found dead in the trunk of a car on the southwest side of Chicago. Badly beaten, they also had their throats slit. Though Spilotro was indicted for his role in what the press popularized as the "M&M Murders," Spilotro was eventually acquitted of the charges. After his acquittal, Spilotro's reputation grew within The Outfit, and his bosses realized he could get information from anyone. A year later he was rewarded when the Chicago Outfit designated him a "Made Man." Spilotro got assigned a territory on Chicago's Northwest side where he controlled The Outfit's bookmaking operations.

In 1971, Spilotro replaced Marshall Caifano as The Outfit's point man in Vegas, another pint-sized tough guy who fit right in as The Mob's third overseer in Vegas. The press gave Spilotro the moniker "Tony the Ant" after agent Roemer referred to him as "that little pissant." The media decided Roemer's word was inappropriate for public consumption and shortened it to the "Ant." Tony Spilotro was also nicknamed "Tough Tony." Spilotro set himself up in Jay Sarno's Circus Circus, purchasing the lucrative gift shop for $70,000. In this way he would appear legitimate, and he'd be almost next door to Rosenthal and the Stardust operations. He took the name of Anthony Stuart, his wife's surname, and under the guise of a legitimate businessman, began his nefarious criminal activities. By 1974 Spilotro had sold the gift shop at Circus Circus for $700,000, ten times the price he had paid for it.

It wasn't long after Spilotro's arrival in Las Vegas that five murders occurred. Each victim was a loan shark, and curiously, each had been tortured before being killed and buried in the desert.

SPILOTRO AND ROSENTHAL

Noted odds-maker extraordinaire Frank Rosenthal was first linked to Spilotro in 1962, when Spilotro pleaded guilty to attempted bribery of a collegiate basketball player. The two mobsters worked together in Miami in 1964, when Spilotro was sent there to oversee Rosenthal's bookmaking business and make sure no one muscled in on The Outfit's operations. The former boyhood buddies from Chicago became acquainted again in Las Vegas, when Rosenthal began running the operations of the Stardust, Fremont, Hacienda, and Castaways for The Outfit.

OPERATION VEGMON

William F. Roemer Jr. was the lead FBI case agent working "Operation VEGMON" (Vegas Money), which followed the trail of the skim money from Las Vegas back to the Midwest. The courier for the wise guys was Ida Devine, the wife of a wholesale meat proprietor who supplied Outfit casinos with choice cuts of steaks and chops. To maintain goodwill and keep his business intact, the meat supplier sanctioned the scheme to have his wife transport the skim from Las Vegas to the Chicago law firm of Bieber & Brodkin, long-time mouthpieces for The Outfit.

From Las Vegas Ida Devine traveled by train and was given the best accommodations at the Ambassador East Hotel, while Bieber & Brodkin divvied the cash among the appropriate people—sweet operation for both the businessman and the Chicago wise guys. Neither the courier, nor her husband, was ever prosecuted for their questionable activities.

The tough-guy reputation Spilotro acquired was well deserved. In addition to the 25 murders in the Chicago area alone that the FBI linked him to, one was a particularly grisly torture and killing of local enforcer and loan shark William "Action" Jackson, whom The Outfit suspected of cooperating with federal authorities. According to Roemer, Jackson "was hung on a meat hook while being slowly tortured to death." [90]

THE HOLE IN THE WALL GANG

In 1976, Spilotro formed a burglary ring with his brother Michael and with Herbert "Fat Herbie" Blitzstein, utilizing eight other associates as well. The crew became known as the Hole in the Wall Gang because of its modus operandi for gaining entry—drilling through exterior walls and ceilings. Also in 1976, together with Chicago bookmaker Blitzstein and brother Michael, Spilotro opened The Gold Rush, Ltd, a combination jewelry store and electronics factory located one block from the Strip. It served the gang as a place to fence stolen goods.

By 1979, things went from bad to worse for the Vegas enforcer. Gaming authorities added his name to the infamous Nevada Black Book, barring him from stepping foot in every casino in the state. Spilotro was outraged by the ruling, though it didn't stop him from further criminal activity. Away from Nevada casinos, Anthony Spilotro continued loan sharking, stealing, and fencing stolen goods.

To make matters worse, after his own arrest for an attempted burglary at Bertha's Jewelry store in Las Vegas, Spilotro's boyhood friend Frank Cullotta turned federal witness to save himself when he realized Spilotro was out to kill him. Cullotta admitted that for many years he'd done "muscle work" on Spilotro's behalf including setting up the infamous 1962 M&M murders of Miraglia and McCarthy.

More heat for Spilotro came when Sal Romano, a crew member who specialized in disabling alarm systems, flipped and became a government informant. Then, during the July 4, 1981, burglary at Bertha's Jewelery, Romano worked counter-intelligence. FBI Agent Roemer wrote, "Unbeknown to Spilotro, his brother Michael, partner Herbie Blitzstein, and the Hole in the Wall Gang burglars, Romano had turned informant several months earlier; federal agents and police were waiting for the burglars when the heist at Bertha's went down."[91]

DEATH OF ANTHONY SPILOTRO

Unfortunately for Anthony Spilotro, his once-reliable value as a Vegas point man had become a security risk to his underworld bosses. He was indicted in Las Vegas for heading a burglary ring. Moreover, he violated Mob decorum by initiating an affair with Geri, the wife of Frank Rosenthal. It was also rumored that he was dealing drugs. Meanwhile, though Frank Cullotta had testified against Spilotro, his testimony was found insufficient, and Spilotro was acquitted of murder charges.

Anthony Spilotro, whose affair with Geri sabotaged his friendship with Rosenthal, ultimately met his demise at the hands of mob killers. As portrayed in the film *Casino*, Spilotro and his brother Michael were buried in a corn field in Enos, Indiana. According to the *Chicago Tribune*, Nicholas Calabrese, a former Mob hit-man who "testified in the Operation Family Secrets trial, said the brothers were told they were being promoted in The Outfit. Anthony Spilotro was to become a 'capo,' and his brother Michael was to become a 'made member.' They were driven to a Mob home in Bensenville, Illinois, and were beaten to death in the basement. Later they were transported to the Indiana cornfield."[92]

At the time of his death, Anthony Spilotro was 48. Anthony Spilotro was ultimately replaced in Las Vegas by Donald "The Wizard of Odds" Angelini. Anthony Spilotro was survived by his wife Nancy, his son Vincent, and his remaining brothers.

* * *

Chapter 12

MEMORABLE LAS VEGAS CELEBRITIES OF THE MOB ERA

*P*icture sitting front stage at the Desert Inn's Copa Room enjoying such great celebrities perform as Frank Sinatra, Dean Martin and Sammy Davis Jr. Imagine too, seeing Elvis Presley, the soon-to-be king of rock 'n' roll, perform live at the New Frontier as a 21-year old teen idol. If you were lucky enough to be in Las Vegas from 1956 through the early 1960s, you had the opportunity to see these great performers live, on stage, for the mere price of a two drink minimum. These were the old days—the days when The Mob ran Las Vegas.

FRANK SINATRA: OL' BLUE EYES WAS A LAS VEGAS LEGEND

From his first gig in September 1951 at Wilbur Clark's Desert Inn, until his last performance at the MGM Grand in May 1994, Ol' Blue Eyes was a Las Vegas legend for nearly 43 years. Along with his "Rat Pack" cronies, Sinatra introduced an era of "cool" to Las Vegas at a time when resort owners were walking around in cowboy hats.

Recalling Sinatra's influence on Vegas, Lorraine Hunt, former entertainer and Lt. Governor of Nevada, once said, "All these guys came in with their mohair tuxes and the black satin shoes. That look was so cool. I remember being a teen-ager I was so attracted to those shiny shoes. Prior to Sinatra, we were more of a Western-feeling town,"[93] said Hunt. Sinatra brought style and sophistication to the Strip. "That Sinatra aura brought international royalty, and made us a global destination. It was a simpler day in a smaller town, and Sinatra's magic was more easily described: gambling, womanizing, drinking till dawn—and all of it with style,"[94] added Hunt in an interview with the *Las Vegas Review-Journal*.

Sinatra's legacy would be lacking without the great impresario Jack Entratter, the driving force behind one of the defining casinos of the early Las Vegas Strip—the Sands. Entratter was a showman and producer par excellence. In 1946, Entratter became general manager of New York's Copacabana club. A year later he owned stock in the club and within three years held controlling interest. In 1952, the 38-year-old Entratter cashed out to become general manager of a new carpet joint just opening on the Strip that was called the Sands. He established the Sands as one of the hottest entertainment spots in the country.

Playing the Sands' Copa Room could not have come at a better time for Sinatra. His first gig in Las Vegas had been less than favorable. He was in the midst of a nationwide scandal after leaving his wife, his childhood sweetheart, Nancy, for Ava Gardner. The young sensation from Hoboken, New Jersey, was a virtual has-been by the age of 34. Sinatra had risen to the top since singing for the Tommy Dorsey and Harry James bands in 1939. His smooth style and distinctive voice, which blended with his boyish charm, made him a super star among the bobbysoxers who packed New York's Paramount theatre during World War II.

By war's end, Sinatra's popularity seemed to stabilize. Yet, by the end of the forties, his career had totally tanked. His records with Columbia weren't selling, his movies weren't popular, and the bobby-soxers no longer crowded his live performances.

1949: A ROCK-BOTTOM YEAR

For Frank Sinatra, the year 1949 had to be the absolute pits: an all time low in his legendary career. He was fired from his radio show and six months after that his New York concerts failed miserably. Columbia Records wanted out of its contract with him. Then, in 1950 MGM released him from his film contract. Worse, his own agent, MCA fired him.

173

Sinatra's debut in Las Vegas took place at the Desert Inn on September 4, 1951, just a few days after a reported suicide attempt in Lake Tahoe by Sinatra. Both the crooner and local authorities quickly discounted the incident, calling it a sleeping pill miscalculation: others insinuated Ava baiting. The crooner's long-time valet, George Jacobs, the man who found Sinatra in a stupor, said otherwise. Years after the incident in *My Way*, Kitty Kelley quotes Jacobs as confirming that Sinatra did try to commit suicide over Ava Gardner that night. "'Thank God, I was there to save him,' Jacobs said. 'Miss G. was the one great love of his life, and if he couldn't have her, he didn't want to live no more.'"[95] To make matters worse, in a short period of 23 months Sinatra divorced, remarried, and was almost divorced again.

But eventually good things started to happen for Sinatra. His debut at the Sands on October 4, 1953, was very successful. Six months later, he earned a Best Supporting Actor Oscar for his role as Maggio in the acclaimed film *From Here to Eternity*, which elevated his career even more. Fortunately for the hard-working crooner, he saved himself. When he read the script *From Here To Eternity* he knew the part of Maggio, the tough little Italian who refused to be broken, was written for no one but him.

It was Ava Gardner, who at the time was devoted to Sinatra, helped him get the Maggio role. As the story goes, she went directly to Joan Cohn, the wife of Harry Cohn, head of Columbia Pictures. Ava pleaded with Joan to talk her husband into giving Frank a screen test. Frank was perfect for the part of Maggio, Ava said, which Harry would realize once he saw the screen test. Despite the inappropriate nature of the request, Ava impressed Joan with her devotion to her husband. Joan agreed to talk with Harry and to keep Ava's involvement secret.

The role of Maggio came at a low point in Frank's career and he desperately wanted the part. However, Harry Cohn felt Sinatra was nothing more than a washed up, has-been crooner. Eventually Cohn agreed to the screen test, whether as a result of Joan's pleas or Sinatra's refusal to take no for an answer. Sinatra tested ahead of five other actors, among them Eli Wallach, and won the part. Once Columbia pictures producer Buddy Adler saw Frank Sinatra's performance he had no interest in testing anyone else. After his screen test, Frank Sinatra was in; Adler never even looked at the other five candidates, and the rest is history.

Within a few months Sinatra was back on his feet making *Guys and Dolls, The Tender Trap,* and *The Man With the Golden Arm.* During his colorful career Sinatra made 20 feature films. His renewed momentum in cinema carried over to his recording career, too. After leaving Columbia, Capitol Records signed him to a new recording contract, and his singing became better than ever, with three consecutive million-record sellers. Singer Paul Anka said, "Under the arrangement of Nelson Riddle, Sinatra entered into a second, more mature phase in his career." Then, NBC offered him a multi-million-dollar contract for a future unspecified number of television appearances. His Oscar-winning portrayal of the little tough guy, Maggio, brought him the kind of work that had eluded him for years. In a later interview, Sinatra said, "The greatest change in my life began the night they gave me the Oscar. It's a funny about that statue—I don't think any actor can experience something like that and not change."

SINATRA AT THE SANDS

In time, the Sands became Sinatra's playground, largely due to his allegiance to Jack Entratter, who had stood by him through all his troubles, but also due to his financial investment in the casino. Only months prior to winning the Oscar, Sinatra became financially revitalized when, after 14 months of deliberation, he was approved for a Nevada gaming license and bought two percent of the Sands Hotel. His interest in the Sands grew to nine percent—a testament to his popularity, his ability to fill the casino with high rollers, and his relations with the underworld, because the new Strip resort was at that time controlled by more Mafioso than any other casino in Nevada.

Besides Bugsy Siegel's Flamingo, only four other casino-resorts were operating on the Las Vegas Strip, and Sinatra could see the future. He knew the city would eventually become a boomtown for gamblers. It couldn't miss—Las Vegas was the only place in the country that had legalized gambling. In time, his foresight proved correct and eventually made Sinatra a multi-millionaire.

Justice Department files indicate that Sinatra purchased his initial two percent share in the Sands for $70,000. His additional seven percent ownership of the resort was a gift from Vincente "Jimmy Blue Eyes" Alo. The number one underworld man at the Sands was Joseph "Doc" Stacher, a gangster out of

New Jersey, second only to Meyer Lansky in the East Coast Mob. Doc looked on Sinatra as his son. Stacher's police rap sheet included assault and battery, larceny, robbery, hijacking, and investigation for murder. The Sands' official host was Charles "Babe" Baron, once suspected of murder. A few of the unseen mobsters connected to the Sands included Anthony "Joe Batters" Accardo, future boss of the old Capone mob, Joe Fusco, Meyer Lansky, and Abraham Teitelbaum, a former consigliere to Capone.

In 1979 "Doc" Stacher admitted, "The mob had offered Sinatra a share in the Sands so that he would draw the high rollers. To make sure we'd get enough top-level investors, we brought George Raft into the deal. The object was to get him to perform there, because there's no bigger draw in Las Vegas. When Frankie was performing, the hotel really filled up."[96]

Sinatra reigned supreme at the Sands for the next 13 years. He eventually became vice president of the corporation, and when performing in the Copa Room he earned more than $100,000 a week. His drawing power was such that he could do no wrong in the eyes of the "boys." They even built him a three-bedroom suite on the property, including a private swimming pool protected by a stone wall. To satisfy Sinatra's culinary whims, they ordered Italian breads, prosciutto, and provolone that he relished flown in from New York.

When Sinatra performed in the Copa Room, he always opened by saying, "Welcome to my room." Because he filled the house with big-money players, the casino became his kingdom, and he could do what he pleased in it. The Sands gave him $3,000 a night to gamble with, but he regularly went through that amount in ten minutes. The Sands' extended him credit, at times allowing him to play no limit games and frequently ignoring his markers.

To his friends, Sinatra was extremely generous, especially when they came to the Sands. Kitty Kelley wrote, "He 'comped' all of his friends with free food and free drinks for days at a time, and expected each of them to perform at the Sands, exclusively. If they didn't, they were no longer his friends, as Judy Garland found out when she accepted a Las Vegas engagement at another hotel." Garlands' performing elsewhere was "strictly a business deal," but "Frank took it as a personal rebuff." [97]

Frank Sinatra made movies at the Sands, recorded some of his greatest albums, sponsored boxing matches, gave glamorous parties and virtually made it the place to go in Las Vegas. Hank Greenspun, publisher of the *Las Vegas Sun*, wrote in a front page editorial: "He frequently flew in Hollywood celebrities, and crowds jammed the casino just in hope of seeing a star having a drink or placing a few bets." Greenspun added, "When Frank Sinatra was in town, it was the economic equivalent of three conventions."[98]

Gambling to Sinatra was second nature. He grew up in the midst of it. His mother, Dolly, had her own bookie, who regularly aroused the neighbors playing bocce ball, an Italian form of ten pins and challenging truck drivers to five-dollar throws. Early on, he watched his father play poker in weekly games and was exposed to betting on all sports, particularly horse racing and boxing. Sinatra's Uncle Gus ran numbers in Hoboken, and his Uncle Babe reportedly had an extensive police rap sheet for crimes like usury and loan sharking.

Ol' Blue Eyes had begun going to Las Vegas on a regular

basis shortly after he moved to the West Coast, frequently dropping thousands of dollars at the tables. In time, he developed an affinity with the men who ran Las Vegas; he seemed to thrive in the nocturnal environment and gambled with abandon. One night he lost over $50,000 playing baccarat. Sinatra first played the fast, big-money card game in Monte Carlo and became so fascinated by the action that as part owner of the Sands, he insisted the casino start its own baccarat game. At the Sands, Frank Sinatra was known to go up to a baccarat table with $10,000, bet the entire bundle, ride it up to $40,000, lose it, and walk away from the table with hardly a shrug.

GAMING LICENSE REVOKED

By 1963, Frank Sinatra not only held points in the Sands Casino Las Vegas, he became the principal owner of the Cal-Neva Lodge & Casino in Lake Tahoe. In September of that year, after he reapplied for his gaming license, the Nevada Gaming authorities recommended that his gambling license be revoked for allowing Chicago crime boss Sam Giancana a seven-day stay at the Cal-Neva Lodge. The mere presence of the mobster at Cal-Neva was a violation of Nevada law, since he topped the Black Book list of excluded persons not allowed in Nevada casinos.

After giving the issue a lot of thought, Sinatra chose not to fight the Board's revocation order. He surrendered his gaming license and eventually sold his interests in the Nevada casinos for a reported $3.5 million. Kitty Kelley wrote in *My Way*, "Sinatra never could understand the stigma of friendship with Giancana," said Phyllis McGuire, who was Giancana's girlfriend during the controversy. "He'd been friends with the boys for years, ever since he needed to get out of his contract with Tommy Dorsey." [99]

179

McGuire reported in an interview that on several occasions Frank and Dean flew to Chicago and sang free of charge for Sam. She remembers them, including Sammy, performing at Giancana's Villa Venice and at Giannotti's Restaurant and Cocktail Lounge in 1962.

Peter Lawford summarized Sinatra's relationship with The Windy City by saying, "Because of Giancana, he kowtowed to the Chicago mob. Why do you think Frank ended every one of his nightclub acts by singing 'My Kind of Town Chicago Is'?" [100]

Sinatra was also friends with Joe Fischetti, whose friendship dated back to 1938. They ran into each other in November 1947 at the Chez Paree in Chicago and hugged each other like brothers. Sinatra had style, and Fischetti, a distant cousin of Al Capone, was raised in the kind of family whose sense of honor Sinatra admired. Joe Fischetti was amici nostri, Italian for "a made man," someone who had sworn in blood to uphold omertà, the Mafia's code of silence. He was a soldati, a soldier, in the dark society of La Cosa Nostra, or Mafia, an ancient Arabic term meaning "sanctuary."

CHRONICLE OF THE RAT PACK

Over the years several explanations circulated for how the Rat Pack came into being. The name was first used in the 1950s in reference to a group of friends and celebrities, including the young Frank Sinatra. One version claimed that the original group leader was Humphrey Bogart, with Lauren Bacall as the "Den Mother." After observing her husband and his friends enter the house from a night out in Las Vegas, she said words to the effect of, "You look like a goddamn rat pack."

Another version is that "Rat Pack" is a shortened version of "Holmby Hills Rat Pack," Bogie and Bacall's home, which served as a regular hangout. Stephen Bogart said in the TV documentary *Bogart: The Untold Story*, "the original members of the Holmby Hills Rat Pack were Frank Sinatra (pack master), Judy Garland (first vice-president), Lauren Bacall (den mother), Sid Luft (cage master), Humphrey Bogart (rat in charge of public relations), Swifty Lazar (recording secretary and treasurer), Nathaniel Benchley (historian), David Niven, Katharine Hepburn, Spencer Tracy, George Cukor, Cary Grant, Rex Harrison, and Jimmy Van Heusen." [101] In his autobiography *The Moon's a Balloon*, Niven confirmed, "the Rat Pack originally included him but not Sammy Davis Jr. or Dean Martin." [102]

The 1960s version of the Rat Pack, formed after Humphrey Bogart's death in 1957, included Frank Sinatra, Dean Martin, Sammy Davis Jr., Peter Lawford, and Joey Bishop. For a brief period, certain visiting celebrities—Marilyn Monroe, Angie Dickinson, Juliet Prowse, and Shirley MacLaine—were referred to as the Rat Pack Mascots, a designation that apparently made the ladies of the group feel like "one of the boys." The group was as dedicated to drinking as Bogie was. Bogart's principle was, "that the whole world was three drinks behind and it was time it caught up." [103]

The Pack was actually referred to by its members as the Summit, or the Clan, until "clan" became "politically embarrassing, and they hastened to make it known that they had nothing to do with the Ku Klux Klan." [104] The name "Rat Pack" was never called that by any of its members, although it was the term commonly used by journalists and outsiders, and today it remains the enduring name for the group.

In Las Vegas, whenever one of the Pack members was scheduled for a showroom appearance, the rest of the Pack usually came and gave an impromptu performance, which caused much excitement among audiences. Fans swarmed into Las Vegas, and were said to sleep in hotel lobbies or in cars when they could not find rooms so they could experience a Rat Pack performance. The neon marquee of the resorts at which one of them was performing would read, for instance, "SAMMY DAVIS JR—MAYBE DEAN—MAYBE FRANK," although the mainstays of the Pack, Sinatra, Martin, and Davis, could most frequently be found together at the Sands.

Paul Anka, who first played the Sahara in 1959 when he was only 18, was quoted by Kitty Kelley in Sinatra's biography as saying, "Pop music was at its infancy stage and just growing. It was just a bunch of us kids. So, consequently (the casinos) went to these older established acts from the nightclub circuit." [105]

This was an era when television was coming of age, and the way it changed people's habits helped Las Vegas. Instead of going out to supper clubs and seeing shows, Americans started a revolution by staying at home to watch television. That habit put a crunch on supper clubs in other cities, giving Las Vegas the upper hand in presenting established acts. Suddenly, the Pack all came together. "Now you've got the greatest, cool, hippest entertainers around," [106] Anka said of the expanding circle of cool cats – By 1960 it included Dean Martin, who began solo nightclub acts in 1957 after a split with partner Jerry Lewis, and Sammy

182

Davis Jr., the multi-talented sensation of the Will Mastin Trio. Joey Bishop, already established as a solo performer, was reportedly accepted into the Pack as a gag writer and a warm-up for much of the improvised mayhem onstage.

By the late 1950s and early 1960s, these and other stars were the draw pulling audiences to Las Vegas casinos. The budding Strip wasn't sporting theme architecture then as it is today. And the stars came to see Sinatra. Sonny King, a veteran Las Vegas lounge singer, and longtime friend of Sinatra, was quoted as saying: "He was actually the king of Las Vegas, because the minute he stepped in town, money was here. King was also quoted saying, "He drew all the big money people. Every celebrity in Hollywood would come to Las Vegas to see him, one night or another."[107]

In 1960, following on the heels of Frank's acclaimed film *Can Can* was *Ocean's Eleven*, the movie that became the on-screen spectacle for the Pack.

PETER LAWFORD'S FALLING OUT WITH SINATRA

The making of the film *Ocean's Eleven* solidified the mainstay members of the Pack while they filmed it on location in Las Vegas. But events beginning in March 1960, led to major falling out between Frank Sinatra and Peter Lawford. Lawford was the brother-in-law of President John F. Kennedy—dubbed "brother-in-Lawford" by Sinatra—and the Pack actively campaigned for Kennedy by appearing at the 1960 Democratic National Convention. During the convention Lawford asked Sinatra if he would have Kennedy as a guest at his Palm Springs house. According to Kitty Kelley, "Sinatra went to great lengths, including the construction of a helipad, to accommodate the

President.

When Attorney General Robert F. Kennedy advised his brother to sever his ties to Sinatra because of the entertainer's association with Mafia figures, such as Sam Giancana, the stay was cancelled. Lawford was blamed for this, and Sinatra 'never had a good word for him' from that point onward."[108]

Prior to the 1960 Presidential election, Sinatra's daughter Nancy said in a televised A&E documentary, "Her father asked Sam Giancana, because of his ties to the Teamsters, if he could help JFK win the election. Giancana agreed, if in exchange Sinatra would work for nothing in Giancana's night clubs." Many years later Sam Giancana boasted about his contribution to Kennedy's victory. As quoted in Kelley's *My Way*, Giancana frequently told a former Kennedy girlfriend Judith Campbell, "Listen, honey, if it wasn't for me, your boyfriend wouldn't even be in the White House."[109]

Many people credit Sinatra's mobilization of Mob support for getting Kennedy the victory. Years later, the owner of the 500 Club in Atlantic City, Paul "Skinny" D'Amato, claimed that, "Sinatra won Kennedy the election. All the guys knew it."

THE RAT PACK'S HEYDAY

In June 1965, at the height of the Pack's popularity, Sinatra, Martin, and Davis, with Johnny Carson as emcee sitting in for Joey Bishop, who was ill at the time, performed their only televised concert together. It was a closed-circuit fundraiser for Dismas House (the first halfway house for ex-convicts) and was broadcast at the Kiel Opera House in St. Louis. Today that broadcast is available on DVD, as part of the *Ultimate Rat Pack Collection: Live & Swingin.*

A televised interview showed Frank saying that the Pack broke up because each went his way. As for the group's reputation for womanizing and heavy drinking, Joey Bishop said in a 1998 interview: "I never saw Frank, Dean, Sammy, or Peter drunk during performances. That was only a gag! And do you believe these guys had to chase broads? They had to chase 'em away!"[110]

The sixties also saw a major change in ownership of Frankie's favorite stomping grounds, when billionaire tycoon Howard Hughes bought the Sands in 1967. Apparently, under Entratter's liberal accounting policies, the crooner had a substantial line of credit at the casino cage. Not so under management of the new regime. One  night in September Sinatra's credit was cut off, and he reacted by flying into a rage. According to Eleanor Roth, the altercation occurred when Sinatra was refused credit in front of some of the Apollo astronauts visiting the hotel, and he completely lost his temper. Roth said, "When Frank won, he took his cheques, and when he lost, he didn't pay his markers."[111]

"He got up on that table, and started yelling and screaming right in the middle of the casino,"[112] recalled entertainer Paul Anka, who claims to have witnessed the incident. Hotel staff called management and vice president Carl Cohen showed up. He was a big burly guy, but Sinatra threw a punch anyway only to have Cohen return the favor. According to a quote in the *Review-Journal*, "The blow knocked the caps off Sinatra's two front teeth."[113] The rumor mill credited the altercation to Howard Hughes' hatred of Sinatra after Ava Gardner passed up Hughes to marry the singer. Limiting Sinatra's credit in the casino was Howard's way of embarrassing Sinatra and evening the score.

FRANK SINATRA PERFORMS AT CAESARS PALACE

In November 1968, Sinatra signed to perform at Caesars. Two years later casino credit would again, be at issue, and it created more trouble for Sinatra when, as Kitty Kelley describes, "casino executive Sam Waterman pulled a gun on him after another argument over casino credit. Sheriff Ralph Lamb threatened to throw the singer in jail, saying 'I'm tired of the way he has been acting around here anyway.'"[114]

Unbeknownst to Sinatra, an IRS investigation was going on into the relationship between the Mafia and the entertainment industry. Sinatra was among the targets of the IRS surveillance. On September 6, 1970, an IRS agent working undercover on graveyard shift in the cashier's cage at Caesars watched as one of Sinatra's aides came to the window with a large amount of $100 cheques and walked away with $7,500 in cash. The undercover agent had a special interest in Frank Sinatra because for weeks he watched the crooner take vast sums of money in markers—IOUs to the casino—that were not being deducted from his salary or paid back in winnings. The undercover IRS agent discovered that Sinatra was using the casino for petty cash. Whatever he won off a marker, he put it in his pocket, and whenever he ran out of cheques to bet with, he simply signed another marker for $10,000. It was easy money for him, but concern grew about his paying back his markers. Sinatra told friends it wasn't necessary for him to pay his markers, because when he performed at Caesars and then played the gaming tables, he figured he attracted enough big money around him that the casino earned huge profits, larger than they would without him.

The story related in *My Way* went like this. At about five a.m. the undercover agent got a call from the blackjack pit saying that Sinatra had just signed another marker. The agent phoned Sandy Waterman, casino manager, who had been part owner of the Cal-Neva with Sinatra in 1963. Waterman dressed, came down to the casino floor, and was informed of what was going on. He stood quietly in a corner and waited for the next time Sinatra's aide approached the cage window. When he did, Waterman nodded his okay to cash in Sinatra cheques. Then he walked over to the blackjack table to deal with Sinatra.

Waterman said to the singer, "I want $10,000 in markers," recalled the agent.

"What's the matter? My money isn't good here?" asked Sinatra.

"Yeah, your money is good as long as you've got money. You don't get cheques until I see your cash."

The undercover agent continued, as quoted by Kelley. "That's when the trouble started and Frank called Waterman a kike and Sandy called him a son of a bitch guinea. They went back and forth like that in front of a big crowd of people, including three security guards, until Sandy whipped out his pistol and popped it between Sinatra's eyeballs... Sinatra laughed and called him a crazy Hebe... He said he'd never work at Caesars again and walked out... Frank had carte blanche at Caesars—complete run of the casino—but it's getting heavy when you have built up so much in markers and maybe 50 percent of it is petty cash in your pocket. This must have been going on for a long period of time, because Waterman got pretty excited about it,"[115] the agent recalled.

Sheriff Ralph Lamb was irate about the incident. Waterman ended up being booked for pulling a gun. The next day the district attorney dropped the charge against Sanford Waterman. The district attorney was quoted as saying, "My reports indicated Waterman still had finger marks on his throat where Sinatra grabbed him. There seems to be reasonable grounds for making the assumption that Sinatra was the aggressor all the way."[116]

People who knew him reason that Frank Sinatra's crude behavior at Caesars Palace goes back to his growing up years in New Jersey. His first job was with a newspaper, the *Jersey Observer*, where he started out riding news trucks and later was promoted to copy boy. One day he took some of his first wages and bought new clothes. While he strutted about Hoboken showing them off, the cops stopped him, wanting to know where he got them. He reportedly wised off by saying to them, "Ya copper, whats it to you?"[117] With that, he was unmercifully beat up, resulting in a smashed nose, cracked ribs, with his face and body a bloody mess, and his tattered and torn new clothes. From that day on, any kind of authority directed his way made him a little crazy.

SINATRA'S ANNOUNCED RETIREMENT

When sales of his famous signature song "My Way" began to decrease, Sinatra announced his retirement. And so began the longest ever farewell engagement. "The Voice" continued to perform until his 79th year. Sinatra had attempted an earlier retirement in March 1971, citing a desire to spend more time with his family, and perhaps write. He returned in April 1973 to record tracks for the LP *Ol' Blue Eyes Is Back.*

Frank Sinatra performed his final public concerts in Japan's Fukuoka Dome in December 1994. Two months later, he sang at a private party for 1,200 guests on the final night of the Frank Sinatra Desert Classic golf tournament. It was his very last performance. *Esquire Magazine* reported of his show that he was "clear, tough, on the money and in absolute control."[118] His closing song was "The Best is Yet to Come."

Twenty years earlier Sinatra had told *Daily News* columnist Kay Gardella that Billie Holiday, whom he first heard in New York's 52nd Street clubs in the 1930s, was the greatest single musical influence on him.

Frank Sinatra's attitude can be summed up in an anecdote about when Quincy Jones was arranging the album *Sinatra at the Sands* in Los Angeles in 1966. Sinatra had phoned Jones at his hotel room and invited Jones to join him in Las Vegas for a weekend. Jones turned him down, saying he had too much to do. Sinatra said, "Q, you gotta live every day like it's your last because one day you'll be right."[119]

Two other quotes attributed to Sinatra are equally memorable: "You only live once, and the way I live, once is enough." And his closing line to audiences after completing his last song at a live performance, "Thank you for letting me sing for you."

Frank Sinatra passed away on May 14, 1998, at the Cedars

Sinai Medical Center in Los Angeles. He was 82 years old. The following night the lights on the Las Vegas Strip were dimmed in his honor. President Bill Clinton said that he had managed "to appreciate on a personal level what millions of people had appreciated from afar."[120] Singer Elton John added that Sinatra "was simply the best—no one else even comes close."[121]

He was survived by his wife Barbara, whom he married in July 1976, and by his three children from his first marriage to Nancy: Nancy Sandra, born in 1940; Franklin Wayne Emmanuel (Frank Jr.), born in 1944; and Christina (Tina), born in 1948.

FINAL TRIBUTE

"He brought unmatched excitement to the Strip, and defined the word 'swinger' for all times," said actor Gregory Peck at the Las Vegas golf tournament that bears Sinatra's name. Peck added, "With his little gang of merry men he established forever a sense of free-floating fun and frolic that captured the imagination of the world."[122]

In the 1960s, Frank Sinatra played a major role in desegregating Nevada hotels and casinos, leading his fellow Rat-Pack buddies and label mates on *Reprise* in boycotting casinos and hotels that wouldn't allow black singers to play, or that wouldn't allow black patrons entry. Author Stephen Holden wrote, "Sinatra was... the first modern pop superstar.... Following his idol Bing Crosby, who had pioneered the use of the microphone, Sinatra transformed popular singing by infusing lyrics with a personal intimate point of view that conveyed a steady current of eroticism.... Almost single-handedly, he helped lead a revival of vocalized swing music that took American pop to a new level of musical sophistication... his 1950's recordings... were instrumental in establishing a canon of American pop song literature."[123]

In final praise to The Voice, a moniker given the sensational crooner by a talent agency early in his career, the world had never heard anyone like Frank Sinatra before... and likely, never will again!

In the early 1950s when Frank Sinatra was in the midst of a fabulous singing career, an up-and-coming performer named Elvis Aaron Presley was gaining popularity among America's teens for his singing of a new form of music—rock 'n' roll. Sinatra never came to terms with rock 'n' roll; to him that kind of music was deplorable. And he was appalled by the arrival of the former truck driver from Tupelo, Mississippi, who wiggled and shimmied as he sang his rockabilly songs, driving teenage girls into a screaming frenzy unseen since The Voice himself had thousands of bobby-soxers swooning at the Paramount. Sinatra also despised the Elvis "look"—the glittery suits and the blue suede shoes. The crooner sang slow, yearning ballads and damned the rockabilly interloper for transposing these traditional rhythms into sexy rock music.

Perhaps what Sinatra resented most was Elvis's popularity in a new style of music that threatened to surpass his own. By 1956, that's what Elvis did, becoming the undisputed king of rock 'n' roll. Though Ol' Blue Eyes believed that rock music didn't deserve a place on the Top 40 charts, Elvis virtually stayed on top for 30 years.

ELVIS HAD A SPECIAL LOVE AFFAIR WITH LAS VEGAS

Picture the Las Vegas Strip circa late 1960s—most of the big showroom stars of the era had either lost their luster, were too old to perform, or had passed away. Those who survived, other than Frank Sinatra, lacked the drawing power to fill the Strip resorts with tourists.

All that changed in July 1969 when Kirk Kerkorian opened the 1,500 room International Hotel, at the time the largest in the world, and tried to sign a big-time rock 'n' roller such as Elvis Presley to perform in his showroom. Of the new casino resort's three showrooms, the largest was the 2,000-seat Showroom Internationale. Kerkorian envisioned the city's first megaresort would be a city in itself, with a myriad of entertainment choices. He hired a talented casino man, Alex Shoofey, as general manager, and together they tried to induce Elvis to open as their headliner.

The International Hotel's grand opening just happened to coincide with Elvis Presley's departure from his movie career, which had endured over seven years and 33 films that typically featured his choreographed songs. About this time Elvis had started hinting to his manager Colonel Tom Parker that he wanted to go back on the road.

COLONEL PARKER'S INFLUENCE

Naturally, what Elvis wanted was irrelevant when it came to his manager, the "all-seeing" Colonel Parker—who appeared to care more about the singer's career than the singer did. Parker oversaw the details of Presley's rise to fame and fortune with a

192

ferocious dedication. In turn, the Colonel reaped far more than the usual 20 percent management fee, including a whopping 50 percent near the end of Presley's life.

Eventually, Parker took over control of more than Elvis' business' interests—he controlled the way he lived, too. It was the Colonel who insisted that draftee Elvis should carry out all the regular duties of an army recruit. "Parker knew that if Elvis went through basic training, carried his own gear and rifle, marched, and went on guard duty, all just like a normal soldier, that it would help his public image."[124]

While serving in Friedberg, Germany, Elvis met the 14-yearold Priscilla Beaulieu. In her autobiography, Priscilla confirmed that Parker advised Presley that serving as an ordinary soldier would gain popular respect, even though serving in Special Services would enable him to perform and remain in touch with the public.

After years of preventing Elvis from getting married, for fear the singer would lose his teen-idol fans, Parker decided it was time for Elvis to wed Priscilla, whom he had courted over seven years and lived with for several years. When the nuptials took place on May 1, 1967, the Colonel extracted every ounce of publicity from the event—he had his old pal Milton Prell, owner of the Aladdin, host the wedding.

TEEN IDOL TO "VEGAS ELVIS"

For the king of rock 'n' roll, deciding in 1969 to reinvent himself in Las Vegas was difficult. Moreover it was an abrupt decision—a calculated career move. Thirteen years earlier in the spring of 1956, a young teen idol named Elvis Presley debuted at the New Frontier. Parker had booked the budding star to a two-week engagement headlining a show that opened "with the soothing strings of the Freddie Martin Orchestra, followed by the Borscht Belt humor of Shecky Greene,"[125] reported the *Review-Journal.*

When Elvis appeared on stage before a Las Vegas audience for the first time, he was a 21-year-old budding rock star with a ducktail haircut, long sideburns, eye shadow, wearing mostly black, and his pink shirt collar turned up. He was backed by Scotty Moore, Bill Black, and D.J. Fontana. With his guitar draped over his shoulder he snarled those famous lips, then started those hips gyrating and began to sing.

According to biographer Peter Guralnick in *Last Train to Memphis,* "While Elvis was already becoming a great hit with the teens around the country he was not the typical Las Vegas Strip entertainer at the time and was met with a cool reception. After the first performance, at which the audience politely applauded, but showed none of the wild enthusiasm to which they were accustomed to."[126] At that point Scotty, Bill, and D.J. knew they were in for a long two weeks.

Newsweek magazine reported that Elvis's presence in the show was tantamount to a "jug of corn liquor at a champagne party," and noted that the stunned audience sat motionless "as if he were a clinical experiment."[127] By the end of the engagement, Elvis moved from the top to the bottom of the New Frontier's marquee, and vowed never again to play night clubs.

But 13 years later in 1969, Alex Shoofey needed big-name entertainers to headline at the International Showroom, and who was bigger than the king of rock 'n' roll, Elvis Presley? Shoofey offered to let Elvis open the hotel. But Parker thought it too risky and declined on the grounds Elvis had performed only once in front of a live audience in 11 years, his "Comeback Special" for NBC in 1968. He was a little out of practice. Nevertheless he looked every bit Elvis, clad in a skin-tight black leather suit. He sang his repertoire of hit singles and finished with his latest hit song, "If I Can Dream."

STREISAND CHRISTENS THE INTERNATIONAL

Barbra Streisand was chosen to christen the Showroom Internationale and Elvis was there to see her perform. It was wise he did, because the experience gave him insight. She was in marvelous voice, but her overall show was lacking. It didn't have the pizzazz of sparkling sets, jokesters, or an entourage of high-stepping performers to enhance Barbra's act. Elvis realized that for Las Vegas talent, by itself, was not enough.

With bad memories of Presley's last Las Vegas gig, Parker reluctantly signed Elvis to a four-week contract with the International at $100,000 per week. After taking in Barbra's performance, Elvis couldn't help remembering 13 years earlier when he had bombed at the New Frontier. Elvis knew he had to build a new act from scratch and he relished the challenge, though he hated the idea of doing Las Vegas—again.

To help find his self-styled "Las Vegas identity," Elvis began scouting lounges and showrooms, studying entertainers and audiences, looking for ideas to stylize into his own show. He found the prototype in Tom Jones, a then-unknown Welsh singer performing at the Flamingo showroom. Performing while encased in a skin-tight black tuxedo, Jones would step to the edge of the stage and lean far back, arching his upper body in such a way that the audience got a good look at the outline of his genitals. The response from the mostly middle-aged female audience impressed Elvis. They cried, screamed, and threw room keys at Jones's feet. During one raucous late-night show they purportedly jumped from their chairs, ripped off their panties, and threw them at his feet.

Elvis admired Jones's vocal skills, although it was his primitive connection with women in the audience that really got Elvis's attention. Instead of relying on the pivoting hips and jerky undulations of his old act, Elvis would use the fluid movements and other martial arts skills he had mastered in studying karate over the years. In fact, he had earned a second degree black belt. On opening night this new "Vegas Elvis" would be supported by a total of 50 artists: a 35-piece orchestra led by guitarist James Burton, his old five-piece rock band, as well as the voices of two soul groups, the Sweet Inspirations and the Imperials.

ELVIS DEBUTS AT THE INTERNATIONAL

When he stepped onto the stage of the Showroom Internationale, on that special night of July 26, 1969, Elvis launched his new Las Vegas career with the most elaborate arrangement of "Blue Suede Shoes" ever heard. There, in a skin-tight black ensemble, he moved along the stage apron kissing one woman after another, passing out his own sweaty handkerchiefs, then more kissing, pushing the energy level of the performance "to a goose-pimply crescendo."[128] Elvis's debut at the

International Hotel and Casino was a huge success, due largely to its producers Steve Binder, Bones Howe, and particularly, musical director Billy Goldenberg, who backed Elvis's vocals with a full-sized orchestra. From then on, the king would never again perform without a throng of back-up singers and at minimum a 30-piece orchestra.

Newsweek commented, "There are several unbelievable things about Elvis, but the most incredible is his staying power in a world where meteoric careers fade like shooting stars."[129]

When the show ended, Elvis had won over the media and the thirty-and forty-year-olds in attendance. Moreover, he became an overnight superstar—again. Elvis won over the International's top management, too. The next day Alex Shoofey sat down in the showroom with Colonel Parker, and opened the conversation with an offer of a new agreement—for five years.

It was said that the Colonel at first appeared uninterested but signed. Elvis would be paid $1 million a year and appear four weeks twice a year. Biographer Guralnick observed, "Shoofey walked away amazed, calling it 'the best deal ever made in this town.' That was an understatement. Las Vegas showrooms were expected to lose money, and − theoretically − recover it in the casino, "by the time Elvis concluded his first month-long engagement, the showroom had generated more than $2 million. It was the first time a Las Vegas resort ever had profited from an entertainer."[130]

Why would anyone, especially Colonel Tom Parker, known as one of the greatest finaglers in the talent business, sell his hot "new" act for such a pittance? The answer lies in Parker's addiction to gambling. Besides Elvis's weekly salary, the

International provided the Colonel with plenty of perks: luxury accommodations, gourmet fare, transportation in hotel planes and limousines, and the crème de la crème of the whole deal unlimited credit in the casino. Parker usually lost $60,000 to $75,000 a night.

Colonel Tom Parker actually lived in the hotel on the 4th floor from the 1970s to the mid-1980s. When Elvis performed at the International, he lived in the penthouse suite on the 30th floor, room 3000, until his last performance there in December 1976.

FIRST BIG-NAME ROCK 'N' ROLLER TO HEADLINE VEGAS

Unencumbered by the memory 13 years ago of his dismal Las Vegas performance at the Last Frontier, Elvis Presley became the first big-name rock 'n' roller to regularly headline in a Las Vegas showroom. During his first two years at the International, the new, flashier version of Vegas Elvis appeared to go well. He was enthusiastic about his new career and busy experimenting, always trying to improve the show. A noticeable change in Elvis occurred in February 1970—possibly brought on by his increased body weight or inspired by Liberace's flowing capes. One night Elvis stepped onto the stage in his famous white bejeweled jumpsuit. "Besides being adorned with ropes of pearls, beads, and rhinestones, the jumpsuit also featured a large belt buckle of sufficient size to hide his burgeoning belly,"[131] wrote the *Review-Journal*.

The king's weight gain may have been the result of boredom, especially when he was not performing. Or it may have been his chosen diet of fast food. He also consumed huge quantities of powerful pharmaceuticals to overcome his problems. His use of prescription drugs likely began in the 1950s, about the same time his career started to take off. Driving from county fairs to roadhouse gigs for months on end, he survived by napping in the back seat of a car.

A chronic insomniac he certainly had a legitimate need for sleeping pills, and he had to also discover how to stay awake with amphetamines. He grew more sophisticated with his medication when he discovered *The Physician's Desk Reference*, which detailed the chemistry, the effects, and the proper use of every U.S.-made prescription drug. He purportedly memorized the *PDR*, and kept it with him the rest of his life.

It was also reported that dozens of pill bottles, most from the Landmark Pharmacy across the street from the International, bore the names of several different aides Elvis kept on the payroll.

THE "MEMPHIS MAFIA"

The circle of friends Presley constantly surrounded himself with—until months before his death—came to be known as the Memphis Mafia. The group of "guys" included Red West, Elvis's friend and bodyguard since the 1950s, Sonny West, and David Hebler. The guys could be identified by a necklace displaying a gold lightning bolt and the initials TCB, which stood for "Taking Care of Business." While Elvis was onstage, wrote Peter Guralnick, "the guys would be doing just that, combing the hotel and environs, inviting attractive girls to join Elvis in the penthouse for an after-show party."[132]

In July 1976, Vernon Presley—who had begun managing his son's financial affairs—fired the three guys, reasoning a need to lower expenses. Guralnick points out that several observers close to Elvis cited different reasons. One associate, John O'Grady, said the men were fired "because their rough treatment of fans had prompted too many lawsuits." Another Presley associate, David Stanley, said the guys were dropped because they were too outspoken about Elvis's prescription drug dependency.

ELVIS PRESLEY'S LATER LIFE

Years of using too many prescription drugs and suffering from depression, now the singer had another problem: he was consumed with jealousy over his wife's affair with handsome karate instructor Mike Stone. Even worse, it was Elvis who had insisted Priscilla take lessons from the expert martial arts instructor. The estranged Elvis couldn't sleep, so he took more sleeping pills. He became increasingly unwell. Twice during 1973 he overdosed on barbiturates and spent three days in a coma in his hotel after the first incident. Near the end of the year, he was hospitalized, semi-comatose from the effects of Demerol addiction.

His primary physician, Dr. George C. Nichopoulos, said that Presley "felt that by getting drugs from a doctor, he wasn't the common everyday junkie getting something off the street."[133]

Since his comeback in 1969, Elvis had staged more live shows with each passing year, so that by 1973—his busiest schedule ever—he was doing 168 concerts. Even with failing health, the next year he undertook another intensive touring schedule. By this point in his life, Elvis was suffering from multiple ailments, including high blood pressure, glaucoma, and liver damage, each reportedly aggravated and perhaps caused by prescription drug abuse. Many years after his death, Dr.

Nichopoulus re-examined Presley's x-rays and concluded that he was probably suffering from degenerative arthritis, which fueled his addiction to painkillers.

Once at a concert in Detroit guitarist John Wilkinson recounted, "I watched him in his dressing room, just draped over a chair unable to move. So often I thought, 'Boss, why don't you just cancel this tour and take a year off...?' I mentioned something once in a guarded moment, but he just patted me on the back and said, 'It will be all right. Don't you worry about it.'"[134]

Regardless, Elvis continued to play to sellout crowds. His final concert, unknown to him at the time, was held in Indianapolis at the Market Square Arena, on June 26, 1977. His, prescription drug abuse finally compromised his health, and he was found dead in his bathroom at Graceland. The official cause of death was listed as cardiac arrhythmia, although the autopsy listed 11 different narcotics in his system, any one of which would have been lethal enough in a large dose.

Back in Las Vegas, the Colonel wasted no time in "Taking Care of Business," initiating all kinds of post-Elvis merchandising schemes to earn money for himself and the Presley estate. During the three years following Elvis Presley's death, his name and image earned more than $20 million, the most lucrative period in his career.

DEAN MARTIN: THE KING OF COOL

For more than 30 years, Dean Martin was among the most popular celebrities in the archives of Las Vegas. Entertainment history was made in the 1960s when Martin, along with fellow "Rat Pack" cronies Frank Sinatra, Sammy Davis Jr., Peter Lawford, and Joey Bishop all performed their impromptu shows at the famous Sands Hotel.

Throughout the 1970s the Riviera Hotel was home for Dean Martin, as was the new MGM Grand, where he performed on its opening night of December 5, 1973. After Bally's purchased the MGM Grand in 1986, he became a mainstay in its Celebrity Room on the Las Vegas Strip, often televising his famous "Roast" specials there. Dean Martin performed more concerts in Bally's 1400-seat Celebrity Room than any other performer.

Also nicknamed the King of Cool, he not only sang but also did stand-up, and was one of the smoothest comics in the business. Besides being a huge star in Las Vegas and a raucous member of Sinatra's Pack, Martin was also a major star in three other areas of show business: motion pictures, television, and recordings.

EARLY LIFE

Born Dino Paul Crocetti on June 7, 1917, in Steubenville, Ohio, to Italian immigrant parents, Dean Martin was the younger of two sons. He spoke only Italian until he started school at age five. As a teenager he became the target of much ridicule for his broken English. He took up playing drums as a hobby, dropped out of high school in the 10th grade, and got a job as a stock boy in a nearby tobacco shop. Later he got work at a speakeasy behind the tobacco shop, doing everything from delivering bootleg liquor to bartending and dealing blackjack. Martin also worked in a steel mill, and by age 15 had begun boxing as a welterweight.

During his prizefighting years, he billed himself as Kid Crochet and earned a broken nose (which was later straightened), and a scarred lip. And according to Nick Tosches' biography *Dino*, Martin had, "several sets of broken knuckles, a result of not being able to afford the tape used to wrap boxers' hands. Of his twelve bouts he would say 'he won all but eleven.'"[135]

Martin gave up prize-fighting and began singing with local bands calling himself "Dino Martini" after the then-famous Metropolitan Opera tenor Nino Martini. Influenced early in his career by the crooning style of Harry Mills of the Mills Brothers, Dean got his first break singing for the Ernie McKay Orchestra. In the early 1940s he started singing for bandleader Sammy Watkins, who suggested he change his name to Dean Martin.

Martin married Elizabeth Anne McDonald in October 1941 and they had four children. Their marriage lasted only eight years before a divorce in 1949. Gradually, Martin developed his own singing style, but in 1943 he bombed at the Riobamba, a high-class nightclub in New York. However, his failure turned out fortuitous because that night he succeeded Frank Sinatra, the setting for their first meeting and eventual lasting friendship.

Up to that time, according to the *Review-Journal*, "Martin had repeatedly sold 10 percent shares of his earnings for up-front cash. He apparently did this so often he found that he had sold over 100 percent of his income. Such was his charm that most of his lenders forgave his debts, and remained friends."[136]

In 1944 Martin was drafted into the U.S. Army and served a year stationed in Akron, Ohio, until reclassified unfit for military service, and discharged. (His reclassification may have been due to a double hernia, which Jerry Lewis wrote about in his autobiography.) By 1946 Martin was surviving as an East Coast nightclub singer, he never reached the fanatic popularity enjoyed by Sinatra. "He seemed destined to remain on the nightclub circuit," cited the *Review-Journal,* "until he met a comic named Jerry Lewis at the Glass Hat Club in New York, where both men were performing. Martin and Lewis formed a fast friendship, which led to their participation in each other's acts, and the ultimate formation of a music-comedy team." [137]

The pair officially debuted at Atlantic City's 500 Club in July 1946. Surprisingly, they were not well received. After their first performance, the owner, Paul "Skinny" D'Amato, took them aside and warned them that if they did not come up with a better act for the second show, they would be fired. The pair went out behind the club to the alley and huddled, agreeing to "go for broke"—that is, to throw out their pre-scripted jokes and improvise.

When they came out for the second show, Martin sang while Lewis, dressed as a busboy, dropped plates and made a shambles of both Martin's singing and the club's sense of decorum, with Martin pelting Lewis with bread rolls and chasing him off stage. Other skits as part of the night's performance included old vaudeville jokes and lots of improvised slapstick humor. The second show of the evening turned out to be a big hit, with the audience members doubled over in laughter. This success led to several other well-paying engagements that culminated in a triumphant run at New York's Copacabana. Essentially, the act consisted of Martin singing and Lewis heckled him, which typically ended up with the pair having fun themselves as they chased each other around the stage. In a later interview, both said their secret was ignoring the audience and playing to one another.

In 1949 the comedic duo had started doing a radio series. The same year Paramount signed Martin and Lewis as comedy relief for the movie *My Friend Irma*. By the early 1950s, they were the hottest act in America. But frustration set in for the pair with the formulaic similarity of the Martin and Lewis movies, which producer Hal Wallis stubbornly refused to change, as Lewis recalled in his book *Dean & Me*. Martin's dissatisfaction ultimately turned to escalating disagreements with Lewis. Eventually they would no longer work together, and the act broke up in 1956, ten years to the day from their first actual teaming.

SOLO CAREER

In 1957, Martin's first solo film, *Ten Thousand Bedrooms*, was a box office failure. Though still popular as a singer, the era of the pop crooner was waning as rock and roll music surged in popularity. For a while it looked as if Martin's career would be relegated to performing at night clubs and being remembered as Jerry Lewis's former partner. But all that changed when Martin replaced actor Tony Randall as co-star of a war film, *The Young Lions*. As a result, Martin's role in the movie began a spectacular comeback. More success followed when Martin starred alongside Frank Sinatra for the first time, in the highly acclaimed 1958 drama *Some Came Running*. By the mid 1960s, Martin was a top movie-recording- nightclub star.

Also in the late 1950s and early 1960s, Dean Martin and Frank Sinatra became close friends. The two of them, along with Sammy Davis Jr., Peter Lawford, and Joey Bishop, formed the legendary Rat Pack. The Pack called themselves "The Summit," made films together such as *Ocean's Eleven*, and formed an important part of the Hollywood social scene in those years.

The Pack was celebrated in Las Vegas, too, especially for their performances at the Sands Hotel. They always wore tuxedos in their act, which usually consisted of singing individual numbers, duets, and trios, and lots of improvised slapstick and chatter. Much of their humor revolved around Sinatra's infamous womanizing and Martin's legendary drinking, as well as cracks about Davis's race and religion. With Davis famously practicing Judaism, he used Yiddish expressions on stage that elicited much hilarity from both stage-mates and audiences. Significantly, Martin and Sinatra refused to perform anywhere that barred Davis, and they were largely responsible for getting Las Vegas casinos to open their doors to African American entertainers and patrons and helped to erase restrictive covenants against Jews.

Despite Martin's reputation as a heavy drinker, he was said to be remarkably self-disciplined. At parties he was often the first to call it a night, and when not on tour or a film location liked to go home to see his wife and children. He also had very strict rules when it came to performances. Phillis Diller said "He borrowed the lovable-drunk shtick from Joe E. Lewis, but his convincing portrayals of heavy boozers in *Some Came Running*, and Howard Hawks's *Rio Bravo* led to unsubstantiated claims of alcoholism. More often than not, Martin's idea of a good time was playing golf or watching TV, particularly westerns."[138]

ALLEGED MOB CONNECTIONS

Some written sources alleged that Martin, early in his

career, had links to the Mafia. Michael Freedland's biography titled *Dean Martin: King of the Road* suggested that Martin was aided in his singing career by The Chicago Outfit. They owned saloons in The Windy city, and later when Martin became a star he performed in their saloons as payback to these bosses—Sam Giancana and Joe Accardo. Freedland also wrote that "while in Las Vegas, Martin was friendly with many mobsters, though not in business with them. Many Vegas entertainers knew the wise guys and were cordial with them personally, without criminal involvement."[139]

A book by John L. Smith, *The Animal in Hollywood*, portrayed Martin's longtime relationship with mob bosses Johnny Rosselli and Anthony Fiato. Smith wrote that "Fiato, aka 'the Animal' did Dean Martin many favors, such as getting back money from two swindlers who had cheated Elizabeth Martin, Dean's ex-wife, out of thousands of dollars of her alimony."[140]

As Martin's career flourished into the 1960s, he both starred in and co-produced a series of four Matt Helm super-spy comedy adventures. A fifth in the series was scheduled, co-starring Sharon Tate with Martin in a dual role, one as a serial killer, but because of Tate's murder and the decline of the spy genre, the film was shelved.

In 1965, NBC launched the weekly comedy-variety series, *The Dean Martin Show*, which exploited his public image as a lazy, carefree boozer. The drinks he consumed, as with his Rat Rack days, were said to be apple juice, though some believed otherwise.

By the 1970s his record albums continued to sell well, even though he was no longer a Top 40 hit-maker, and his weekly television show still earned solid ratings. Meanwhile, in Las Vegas he continued to headline on marquees, guaranteeing casinos standing-room-only crowds wherever he performed. The King of Cool also found a way to make his passion for golf profitable by offering his own signature brand of golf balls. Shrewd investments during his later years substantially increased Martin's personal worth. Friedland's biography of Martin noted that, "At the time of his death, Martin was reportedly the single largest minority shareholder of RCA stock. Martin even managed to cure himself of his claustrophobia by reportedly locking himself in the elevator of a tall building and riding up and down for hours until he was no longer panic-stricken."[141]

LATER LIFE

In 1972 Martin filed for divorce from his second wife, Jeanne. A week later he dissolved his business relationship with the Riviera amid reports that the casino refused Martin's request to perform only once a night. He quickly signed on with the MGM Grand and agreed to a three-year picture deal with MGM Studios.

One year later, two months before his 56th birthday, Martin wed 26-year-old Catherine Hawn. That marriage ended in divorce in November 1976. About this time, Martin reconciled with Jeanne, though they never remarried. That same year he also made a public reconciliation with his one-time partner Jerry Lewis on Lewis's Labor Day Muscular Dystrophy Association telethon that same year.

While flying with the California Air National Guard, Martin's son, Dean Paul, died in March 1987 when his F-4 Phantom II jet fighter crashed. One year later, a much-touted tour with Sinatra and Davis sputtered. Freedland notes that on one occasion, he infuriated Sinatra by asking, "Frank, what the hell are we doing up here?" Martin, always responded best to a club audience and felt lost in the huge stadiums that Sinatra insisted they perform in. Freedland adds that Dean was not the least bit interested in drinking until dawn after their performances."[142]

Martin's final Las Vegas performances were at Bally's in 1989. It was there he reunited with Jerry Lewis on his 72nd birthday for their last performance together. Both of Martin's last two appearances on television involved tributes to his former Rat Pack cronies. He attended Sammy Davis's 64th birthday celebration in May 1990, only a few sad weeks before Davis died from throat cancer. Then in December 1990, Martin congratulated Frank Sinatra at his televised 75th birthday special.

By 1991, Dean Martin had unofficially retired from performing. He never fully recovered from losing his son. To make matters worse, he also suffered for many years from emphysema. As Freedland wrote in his biography of Martin, "Except for nightly visits to his favorite Los Angeles restaurants which lasted until 1995, he kept his private life to himself, emerging briefly for a public celebration of his 77th birthday with friends and family." [143]

Not long before that, in 1993, Martin had been diagnosed with lung cancer, and told surgery was needed on his liver and kidneys to prolong his life. He refused. Martin died on Christmas morning of 1995 at age 78. By his side were ex-wife Jeanne and other family members. That night, lights of the Las Vegas Strip were dimmed in his honor.

SAMMY DAVIS JR: A GREAT ONE-MAN SHOW

Sammy Davis Jr. made his Las Vegas debut as part of the Will Mastin Trio at the El Rancho Vegas in 1945, before headlining as a top showroom act at the Last Frontier. "Sammy is definitely a one-man show," wrote *Las Vegas Sun* critic Ralph Pearl, noting, "Davis could sing, pound out drum solos, reprise a Bill Robinson tap routine, and play a variety of instruments in a rousing 'Birth of the Blues.'"[144] Throughout his phenomenal career, Davis amazed fans, critics, and fellow entertainers with his ability to sing, dance, and play numerous musical instruments.

EARLY LIFE

Samuel George "Sammy" Davis Jr. was born in December 1925 in Harlem, New York, and raised by his paternal grandmother. His parents were vaudeville dancers, but they split up when Sammy was three years old. His father, not wanting to lose custody of his son, took him on tour, where the child learned to dance from both his father and "uncle" Will Matsin. Davis became a skilled dancer and eventually joined the act that became the Will Mastin Trio. Davis once said in an interview that while he was young Mastin and his father shielded him from racism. Snubs, for instance, were explained as jealousy.

However, Davis noted in his autobiography that, when he served in the U.S. Army during World War II he was confronted by strong racial prejudice. "Overnight the world looked different. It wasn't one color any more. I could see the protection I'd gotten all my life from my father and Will. I appreciated their loving hope that I'd never need to know about prejudice and hate, but they were wrong. It was as if I'd walked through a swinging door for eighteen years, a door which they had always secretly held open.'"[145]

Davis served in an integrated Special Services unit with the army, finding that the spotlight lessened the prejudice. "My talent was the weapon, the power, the way for me to fight. It was the one way I might hope to affect a man's thinking,"[146] he wrote. As an African American, Davis endured racism throughout his lifetime. In one later-in-life incident Davis was on a golf course with Jack Benny, when he was asked what his handicap was. "Handicap?" he quipped. "Talk about handicap— I'm a one-eyed Negro Jew."[147] In time, this statement became a signature line, recalled in his autobiography.

SOLO CAREER

After his discharge at war's end, Davis rejoined the family trio, which at the time was performing at clubs around Portland, Oregon. Soon, Davis began to achieve success on his own and was singled out for praise by critics. Several albums of his were produced which led to his 1956 appearance in the Broadway play *Mr. Wonderful.*

When Davis debuted in Las Vegas, like other African-American performers he was allowed to entertain but usually not allowed to stay at the same hotels, gamble in the casinos, nor dine or drink in the resort restaurants and bars. In his autobiography, *Yes, I Can,* Davis wrote, "Black performers entered and exited through kitchens, and sometimes were lucky to get a meal at the places where they performed. They stayed in boarding houses or motels in racially segregated West Las Vegas.

No dressing rooms were provided for black performers and they waited outside by the swimming pool between acts."[148]

Davis had to endure more than racism and bigotry in Las Vegas. While headlining at the Last Frontier in 1954, Davis made a late-night car trip to Los Angeles for a recording session. His friend Charles Head drove the car while Davis stretched out on the back seat to get some sleep. The trip ended in a horrible collision near San Bernardino. Davis lost his left eye, got a broken jaw, and had other facial injuries. He recovered at the Palm Spring's home of Frank Sinatra, where he was told by his older host, "Relax—You're going to be bigger than ever, Charley,"[149]—Sinatra's nickname for Davis.

Eventually, Davis was fitted for a glass eye, which he wore the rest of his life. While in the hospital, his friend Eddie Cantor described to him the similarities between the Jewish and black cultures. Inspired by Cantor's beliefs, Davis, who was born to a Catholic mother and Protestant father, began studying the history of the Jews and years later converted to Judaism.

Sinatra's prophecy seemed to come true, because the car crash marked a turning point in Davis's career. Overnight he changed from a well-known entertainer to a national celebrity. He recovered and returned to perform as a solo act on Las Vegas, Reno, and Lake Tahoe stages, and appeared on Broadway and in films.

In 1959, Davis became a member of Sinatra's celebrated Rat Pack. He was initially denied residence at the Sands Las Vegas, until Sinatra threatened to pull the plug on Rat Pack performances unless Davis got his own suite. In due course, Nevada resort owners gave in to the demands of both Sinatra and Dean Martin, opening the doors for other black entertainers who had been forced to find accommodations in West Las Vegas. When performing in the Lake Tahoe area, he enjoyed staying in a home that casino owner Bill Harrah built to accommodate guest entertainers during their engagements.

As Davis's career progressed, he refused to work at places that practiced racial segregation. His demands eventually led to the integration of Miami Beach nightclubs. In 1964 at the height of his fame, Davis was starring on Broadway in *Golden Boy* every night and simultaneously shooting his own New York-based afternoon talk show during the day. On a rare day off from the theater, Davis typically spent time in the studio recording new songs or performing live, as far away as Miami, Chicago and Las Vegas, or doing television variety specials in Los Angeles. Later, in his autobiography, Davis wrote, "I knew that I was cheating my family of my company, but could not help myself; because I was incapable of standing still."[150]

LATER CAREER

Although still a big draw in Las Vegas, by the late 1960s Davis's musical career began to decline. Even so, his "I've Gotta Be Me" reached #11 on the *Easy Listening* singles chart in 1969. In an effort to reconnect with younger listeners, he recorded some embarrassing "hip" musical efforts with the Motown label. Then, just when his career reached its nadir, he had an unexpected hit with "Candy Man," the theme song from the television series *Baretta* (1975-1978).

Though "Candy Man" was his last recorded Top 40 hit, he remained a live act beyond Las Vegas, occasionally landing television and film parts, including cameo visits to *All in the Family* in which he planted a kiss on the cheek of Archie Bunker, played by Carroll O'Connor, and on *Charlie's Angels* with wife Altovise Davis. He also guest starred in other television shows, including *I Dream of Jeannie* and *The Patty Duke Show*.

Davis admitted to watching daytime soaps, which led to his making a cameo appearance on *General Hospital.* Later he portrayed the recurring character Chip Warren on *One Life to Live*, for which he received a Daytime Emmy nomination in 1980.

Among his many talents, Davis was also an enthusiastic gun owner. He participated in fast-draw competitions, and was capable of drawing and firing a Colt single action revolver in under a quarter of a second. Additionally, he was adept at fancy gun spinning and often appeared on television showing off his skill. Davis also appeared in western films and as a guest star on several "Golden Age" television westerns.

Davis led a controversial life, which seemed to come to a head when he married white, Swedish-born actress May Britt in 1960. The marriage produced one daughter and two adopted sons. They divorced in 1968. He received hate mail while starring in the Broadway production of *Golden Boy* from 1964 to 1966, a role for which he received a Tony Award nomination for Best Actor. At the time, interracial marriages were forbidden by law in 31 U.S. states, and only in 1967 were those laws ruled unconstitutional by the U.S. Supreme Court. Davis's interracial relationship cost him billing at President John F. Kennedy's inaugural ball in 1961, because of concerns about Davis's "illegal" marriage and the political fallout for Kennedy.

Davis began dating Altovise Gore, a dancer in *Golden Boy*, and they eventually married in May 1970, ten years after his first marriage. They adopted one child and remained married until Davis's death in 1990.

Due to surgery for hip replacement, Davis missed a Rat Pack reunion at the new Thomas & Mack Center in 1983, but returned in 1985 with renewed energy to headline at the Desert Inn. Another hip surgery forced him to ease his workload, and he teamed with comedian Jerry Lewis to perform at Bally's Hotel-Casino. The pair also performed in a successful 1988 HBO special, *An Evening with Sammy Davis Jr. & Jerry Lewis.*

After reuniting with Rat Pack pals Sinatra and Martin in 1987, Davis toured internationally with them and Liza Minnelli. His last performance was at Harrah's Lake Tahoe in 1989, the night before his first radiation treatment. He died May 16th, 1990, at his home in Beverly Hills, California. He was 64 years old.

When Davis died he was in debt to the IRS, and his estate was the subject of several legal battles. After Frank Sinatra learned of Altovise Davis's financial troubles, he reportedly gave Davis's widow $1 million in cash.

Davis wrote in his *Yes I Can,* "Being a star made it possible for me to get insulted in places where the average Negro could never hope to go and get insulted."[151] Sammy Davis Jr. became the first of the legendary Rat Pack to die, leading to many tributes in his name in Las Vegas and elsewhere. "In Reno, William Harrah named his main showroom in Davis's honor, and today it is still known as Sammy's Showroom. In Las Vegas, Davis was honored in a manner reserved for only a handful of the most prominent entertainers in Las Vegas showroom history. Marquees and neon lights were dimmed along the Strip in testament to Davis's unmatched skills as a singer, dancer, and all-around entertainer."[152]

* * *

Chapter 13

HOWARD HUGHES
USHERS IN
THE CORPORATE YEARS

While Jimmy Hoffa had supplied the Vegas Mob with Teamster loans in the late 1940s and 1950s, billionaire Howard Hughes in 1967 would fuel a corporate era in Vegas, acquiring a multitude of casinos and other business interests throughout Nevada. Later on others followed, as self-made corporate men such as Steve Wynn and Kirk Kerkorian launched a Las Vegas building boom of billion-dollar mega resorts all financed with junk bonds and stock offerings to the general public through Wall Street.

The story of how the amazing Howard Hughes became Nevada's biggest employer and land owner, and most powerful man during his four-year stint in Las Vegas makes a truly incredible legend. The circumstances that created the legend are even more unusual.

Before the renowned aviator made Las Vegas his home in 1966, he had stayed there several times. On his first visit during World War II he was a guest at the Flamingo, El Rancho Vegas, and Desert Inn. Later in 1953, the then 47-year-old rented a five bedroom cottage near the Desert Inn. He referred to it as the "Green House" because its exterior color contrasted with the sandy-brown desert terrain. During this stopover he acquired 40 square miles of land just northwest of Las Vegas from the Bureau of Land Management (BLM), trading 73,000 acres of land he owned in five northern Nevada counties for the BLM parcel.

Hughes called his newly acquired parcel Husite. He intended to relocate Hughes Aircraft from Culver City, California, to Husite. Maheu noted that Hughes, "had felt oppressed since California levied an income tax in 1935," but that his "key executives and technicians at Hughes Aircraft had flatly refused to be exiled to the desert, and the Husite property remained vacant." The 40-square-mile parcel, vacant for so many years, is today a prosperous master-planned community known as Summerlin.

Hughes lived in the Green House for nearly a year and continued to pay rent with instructions to keep it exactly as it was, despite his never returning there. He frequently visited the Grace Hayes Lodge—today the site of the Mirage—owned at the time by vaudeville headliner/film star Grace Hayes. Hughes reportedly offered to buy the Grace Hayes Lodge, but he declined to continue negotiations when its proprietor countered Hughes' offer with a price of $250,000, ten times what Hughes wanted to pay.

As the years rolled on, the need of Las Vegas for a savior—someone who could cleanse its tarnished Mob image—became apparent. He arrived in the Autumn of 1966, but this time he stayed four years and forever shaped the destiny of Nevada for years to come.

PRIVATE TRAIN FROM BOSTON

On a cold November night in 1966, the reclusive billionaire Howard Hughes and his entourage of business aides made a midnight exodus from the fifth floor of a Boston hotel. Needing peace and quiet, desperate to get away from snooping newspaper reporters and other prying eyes, Hughes boarded a private two-car train and headed west to Las Vegas.

Hank Greenspun, *Las Vegas Sun* publisher and friend to the billionaire, had persuaded Hughes to move to Nevada because of its benefits: no state income tax and lots of land available to a man with money.

Hughes and his entourage arrived in Las Vegas the night on Thanksgiving and were immediately whisked to the Desert Inn, where they occupied the top two floors of penthouse suites. Usually the top floors were reserved for high rollers, but Hughes' aides were a group of non-gambling, Mormon businessmen. Moreover, their reservation was for ten days only at a time when the upcoming holidays would create a large demand for Las Vegas hotel rooms.

Robert Maheu recalled that when he was able to negotiate the rooms at the Desert Inn, the hotel management had not considered the billionaire businessman a high-rolling guest. Ten days passed, and the Hughes' entourage did not check out. With the holidays approaching, Moe Dalitz, owner of the Desert Inn, was furious. New Year's Eve, one of Las Vegas' busiest holidays, was less than a month away, and the suites the Hughes' ensemble occupied had already been promised to high rollers.

ATTEMPTED EVICTION OF HUGHES

Concerned about Hughes' extended stay, Dalitz phoned Maheu and told him that the entire Hughes group must leave or be physically evicted. When Hughes learned of the situation, he told Maheu, "It's your problem—you work it out."[153] So Maheu called in an old favor owed to him by Teamster President Jimmy Hoffa. As the story goes, Dalitz got a call from Hoffa requesting an extension for the Hughes group. Dalitz agreed on the condition that no future extensions would be granted.

The eviction reprieve lasted through the New Year and

several months into 1967. Maheu told Hughes that he had played out his options with Dalitz. "If you want a place to sleep," he said, "you'd damned well better buy the hotel."[154]

The billionaire couldn't have agreed more, and so began Howard Hughes's foray into buying up huge amounts of Las Vegas real estate. Seven months before his Thanksgiving 1966 arrival in Las Vegas, Hughes had been on the defensive over conflict-of interest concerns involving his ownership of both Trans World Airlines (TWA) and Hughes Aircraft. The U.S. federal court forced Hughes to sell his shares in TWA. The sale of his interest in TWA netted him a gross profit of $547 million. Unless he reinvested this huge sum, which the IRS considered "passive income" and taxed at a higher rate than "active" or "working" income, Hughes would lose much of it to taxes.

To most businessmen, negotiating the purchase of a thriving business such as the Desert Inn was the means to an end. To tycoon Howard Hughes, it was crafty deal making. After months of offers and counter offers, Dalitz and Hughes finally agreed on a price of $13.25 million. Once Hughes owned the Desert Inn, he discovered the gross receipts of a casino were considered active income. Overjoyed with the notion of a reduced tax liability, Hughes phoned Maheu. "How many more of these toys are available?" he inquired. "Let's buy 'em all."[155]

Typically, under jurisdiction of the Nevada Gaming Commission, one becomes a licensed operator of a gambling establishment by appearing in person before the commission, undergoing an extensive background check, being photographed and fingerprinted, and filling out financial disclosure papers—all of which Hughes had no intention of doing. The commission, believing the new billionaire resident would be a great asset to the community, bent the rules to accommodate their new reclusive resort owner.

According to K.J. Evans in a *Las Vegas Review-Journal* article, "well-connected Las Vegas attorney Thomas Bell was hired to handle the licensing, and would stay on as Hughes' lobbyist in Carson City. The new governor, Paul Laxalt, persuaded the commission to allow Maheu to appear as Hughes' surrogate." "Laxalt saw Hughes as a better option than the mob," said Maheu. "He was an excellent businessman, and he was totally legitimate—the kind of sugar daddy Las Vegas needed."[156] Finally, in 1967, the Nevada Gaming Commission granted to Hughes the license he needed to operate the Desert Inn.

HUGHES HISTORIC SPENDING SPREE

"The Man," as his close associates referred to their unseen boss, began his historic spending spree from his penthouse atop the luxurious Desert Inn. After acquiring the Desert Inn, Hughes began a roll that boggled the mind of most millionaire gamblers. His next acquisition was the Sands, then a Strip showplace. Its best days when Sinatra and his Rat-Pack pals made the Copa Room their playground, had passed. Even so, when Moe Dalitz was consulted, he told Hughes that the Sands would be a good acquisition. Hughes paid $14.6 million for the casino hotel and 183 acres of prime real estate that, in time, became the Howard Hughes Center.

Hughes then bought the Castaways for $3 million, the Frontier for $23 million, the Silver Slipper for $5.4 million, and the unfinished Landmark, which had stood empty for eight years, for

$17 million. But when Hughes tried to buy the Stardust for $30.5 million, the U.S. Securities and Exchange Commission prevented him from closing the deal, concerned over Hughes holding a monopoly on Las Vegas lodging. "If we had been allowed to buy the Stardust, you wouldn't have had ... all the terrible publicity from that movie *Casino*,"[157] wrote Maheu in *Next to Hughes*.

The Chicago Outfit's emissary to Las Vegas and Hollywood, Johnny Rosselli, approached Maheu one time to tell him who would be the new casino manager. Maheu told him to buzz off. Howard Hughes was not in bed with The Mob, nor did he have any intention of falling in with organized crime. In fact, he was actually working quietly to ease the mobs out of Sin City.

Hughes had to know something to have bought the Desert Inn, Sands, Frontier, Silver Slipper, Castaways, and the Landmark. Acquiring those particular casinos was not an accident. What he knew was contained in a study commissioned by former Attorney General Robert Kennedy, "a blueprint for exorcising the mob from Las Vegas." The study identified the casinos that had to be cleaned up. Maheu wrote that the study said, "the best way to clean them up was by purchase. So you put all the elements together, and who is better equipped with the money than Hughes?" [158]

Casinos were not his only investments in Las Vegas. During his four-year stay Hughes acquired buy options or purchased outright nearly every plot of vacant land from McCarran Airport to Sahara Avenue, a distance of four miles. "We didn't make the new Las Vegas," Maheu said in a 2004 interview. "I like to say we got it ready."[159]

HUGHES BUYS KLAS CHANNEL EIGHT

After Hughes moved into the Desert Inn he realized to his dismay that he couldn't watch movies on late night television, a pastime he enjoyed since his Hollywood days at RKO Studios. A chronic insomniac, he wanted to watch old movies on television when most Las Vegans were either sleeping or out on the town. Metropolitan Las Vegas had no all-night TV stations. In September 1967, *Las Vegas Sun* publisher Hank Greenspun sold his television station, KLAS Channel eight, to Howard Hughes for $3.6 million. Sin City's newest billionaire resident now had his own 24/7 channel to satisfy his late-night addiction.

Hughes' other non-casino properties included the residential lots of the Desert Inn's Country Club, the North Las Vegas Airport, and all the land surrounding McCarran International Airport. His massive portfolio included Harold's Club in Reno, an airline named Hughes Airwest, nearly every vacant lot on the Las Vegas Strip, and some 2,000 mining claims.

When he finished buying up Las Vegas in the autumn of 1970, Hughes' Nevada holdings were worth an estimated $300 million, making him the state's largest employer and the holder of more gaming licenses than anyone else in history!

"JUICED IN"

In the old days of the casino business, it was common practice to "skim" the cash in the counting room from the cash boxes. The purpose, of course, was to illegally avoid paying taxes on some of the gross receipts a casino took in. Another common practice whenever experienced operators purchased a thriving business such as a casino was to remove most of the key personnel and replace them with employees they knew to be

224

trustworthy. If they didn't personally know each prospective employee, someone within the organization had to vouch for them. This practice created the term "juice." Being "juiced in" to a casino meant the person being hired had connections and supposedly could be trusted. In the early days of Las Vegas casinos, "juice" was very important, especially in The Mob-operated joints. Because the people being hired would most likely have access to large sums of money, operators needed assurance that their employees were not thieves.

HUGHES NEGLECTED TO REMOVE THE BANDITS
FROM THE DESERT INN

In 1967, when novice casino operator Howard Hughes took over ownership of the Desert Inn, he unknowingly made the crucial mistake of neglecting to remove the bandits already entrenched there. In one instance, a craps table stayed on the books as closed, yet actually remained open, while the bosses and the dealers continued daily to remove its cash box, and divvy up the booty. It took three months before the oversight was finally discovered. Even more astounding is the revelation that after Hughes death, from 1971 through September 1976, the Hughes holding company, Summa, lost $132 million. Those responsible were said to be the inexperienced people operating Hughes' casinos.

Hughes did not build a single casino in Nevada, "and had at best a rudimentary knowledge of the casino business,"[160] said Robert Maheu, whose *Next to Hughes* cites example after example of the billionaire's missteps. For example, of the six casinos Hughes owned, the most obvious blunder was his purchase of the Landmark, "which both Maheu and Moe Dalitz had strenuously advised against. Though distinctive, it was never a success, and is today a parking lot,"[161]wrote K.J. Evans.

On the other hand, Hughes purchased a thin strip of land, adjacent to Caesars Palace that two decades later became seed money for a young developer's rise to fame and fortune. After Hughes left Las Vegas in 1970, his interest in land waned, and in 1971, he traded that narrow strip of land to a young hopeful named Steve Wynn. Eventually, Wynn sold the land to Caesars Palace and used his profits to buy a controlling interest in downtown's Golden Nugget.

"MORMON MAFIA"

Hughes's massive business holdings were overseen by a small group of aides, most of whom were Mormons. Though Hughes was not a member of their church, they were the only people he found trustworthy enough to handle his business affairs. This group was unofficially dubbed "The Mormon Mafia." In addition to taking care of Hughes' everyday business operations and his health, his aides made every effort to satisfy "The Man's" every whim.

Besides his addictions to movies on late-night television, Hughes was fond of Baskin-Robbins' Banana Ripple ice cream. When that particular flavor was discontinued, his aides sought to secure a bulk shipment for him. The smallest special order Baskin-Robbins would supply was 200 gallons. Fine. The aides had 200 gallons shipped from Los Angeles. Soon after it arrived, Hughes said he was tired of Banana Ripple and preferred Chocolate Marshmallow ice cream. Thus, Desert Inn guests and employees enjoyed free Banana Ripple ice cream for the next 12 months.

While living in his penthouse atop the Desert Inn, Hughes

became concerned about the explosions occurring at the Nevada Test Site only 65 miles northwest of Las Vegas. He tried to stop the explosions but never succeeded in persuading the authorities to halt them. Hughes feared the atomic blasts would frighten tourists and keep them from coming to Las Vegas. He was concerned too, that the rumbles might damage the many structures he owned.

According to the numerous memos he wrote, Hughes envisioned Las Vegas as a model metropolis, with its own high-speed rail, clean water and clean air, mountains on all sides, and cradled in the midst of the Mojave Desert. As a former engineer he also had concerns about sewage draining into Lake Mead, the primary source of drinking water for most Las Vegans.

HUGHES LEAVES LAS VEGAS

After a four-year stay in the city, Hughes was carried out of the Desert Inn on a stretcher, whisked to Nellis Air Force Base in an unmarked van, and flown by private jet to the Bahamas. With his health failing, a bitter corporate struggle broke out over Hughes' immense business and land holdings in Las Vegas. His trusted aide Robert Maheu, personal physician Dr. Robert Buckley, and other top aides were fired once Hughes had been removed from the Desert Inn's penthouse.

The quirky billionaire aviator never returned to his model metropolis, though his strange, almost bizarre legacy continues to nourish the legend of the city's growth and development. Former FBI agent Maheu, Hughes's virtual mouth, eyes, and ears for 13 years, was fired in December 1970 by Chester Davis, the lawyer who defended Hughes in a successful battle over alleged antitrust violations involving TWA, and Summa Executive Vice President

Frank William Gay. Paul Laxalt, then Governor of Nevada, delivered the news to Maheu at the Sands Hotel on December 7. "He told me he had spent over a half hour talking with Howard, and that Hughes had told him that I was fired,"[162] Maheu recalled in *Next to Hughes.*

Once Hughes left Las Vegas in the fall of 1970, his interest in the city diminished. Following his 1976 death, those in control of his estate sold off its casino interests to concentrate on real estate development, namely Husite. It evolved into the planned community development of Summerlin, which was Hughes' real legacy.

DEATH OF THE BILLIONAIRE AVIATOR

Almost five and half years after his abrupt departure from Las Vegas, Howard Hughes at age 70 died on April 5, 1976, in an airplane flying back to Texas where it all began. Two reports, however, told different stories about precisely where his death occurred. One claimed that Hughes died on board an aircraft owned by Robert Graf, en route from Hughes' penthouse in Acapulco, Mexico, to the Methodist Hospital in Houston, Texas. The other claimed he died on board a flight from Freeport, Grand Bahamas, to Houston.

At the time of death, his extensive use of opiates and reclusive activities made Hughes practically unrecognizable. From an imposing 6'2" frame, he weighed barely 90 pounds at the time. His hair, beard, and fingernails were untrimmed. The FBI had to fingerprint the corpse to make a positive identification. When his body was received at the morgue in Houston, an autopsy revealed kidney failure as the cause of death. Severely malnourished, Howard Hughes was already in very poor health at the time of his death. During the autopsy the coroner reportedly found broken hypodermic needles still embedded in his arms. The coroner also noted Hughes other internal organs appeared healthy, although his kidneys were damaged.

Summa executives and heirs began battling over the billionaire's massive estate. William Lummis, the son of a maternal aunt and a Houston lawyer, became Summa's chairman of the board in 1976, and Gay, who presided over Hughes' "Mormon Mafia" of personal aides, became its CEO that same year. Davis remained board director and chief counsel for Summa.

KIRK KERKORIAN—THE QUIET LION

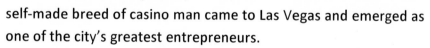

Unlike the eccentric billionaire Howard Hughes, who inherited his money and bought up Nevada casinos like a rich kid in a toy store, a different self-made breed of casino man came to Las Vegas and emerged as one of the city's greatest entrepreneurs.

The story of Kirk Kerkorian, Chief Executive Officer of Caesars Entertainment, which includes the huge $11 billion CityCenter, reads like an all-American rags-to-riches narrative that's hard to put down. His multitude of casino resorts began with the International Casino, developed through expansions and acquisitions, and operates on four continents today. Kerkorian once noted in a rare interview with the *Review-Journal*, "When

229

you're a self-made man you start very early in life. In my case it was at nine years old when I started bringing income into the family. You get a drive that's a little different, maybe a little stronger, than somebody who inherited."[163]

Growing up in Fresno, California, Kirk was the youngest of four children born of Armenian immigrants, Lily and Ahron Kerkorian. In 1922, when he was four-years-old, the family moved to Los Angeles. At age nine he sold newspapers and hustled odd jobs to earn money. He dropped out of school in the eighth grade, and under his older brother's tutelage became a skilled amateur boxer. He fought under the name "Rifle Right Kerkorian" and won the Pacific amateur welterweight championship.

KERKORIAN MEETS TED O'FLAHERTY

In autumn 1939 at age 22, Kerkorian experienced a defining moment in his early career when he met Ted O'Flaherty. Kerkorian started by helping O'Flaherty install wall furnaces, earning 45 cents an hour. "Some days," reported the *Review-Journal*, "Kerkorian would go with him to Alhambra Airport and watch him practice maneuvers in a Piper Cub airplane. Originally disinterested, Kerkorian consented one day to go aloft with O'Flaherty."[164] In the air, Kerkorian discovered he could see the beauty of the mountains on one side and the blue Pacific Ocean on the other. It's when he fell in love with flying.

"He was sold on it right then," O'Flaherty later recalled. "He had never been up in a plane before. But I'm telling you, after that first flight he went right at it. The very next day, he was back out at the field to take his first flying lesson."[165]

In 1940, Kerkorian sensed America would inevitably be drawn into the war in Europe, so he decided to become a licensed aviator before he got drafted into the infantry. One day he arrived at a desolate airfield in the middle of the Mojave Desert called "The Happy Bottom Riding Club," adjacent to the USAF's Munroc Field, now Edwards Air Force Base. A combination flight school and dairy farm, it was owned by pioneer aviator Florence "Pancho" Barnes. There, Kerkorian received flying lessons in exchange for milking her cows and tending the cattle.

"I haven't got any money," Kerkorian told Barnes. "I haven't got any education. I want to learn to fly. I don't know how I can do it. Can you help me?"[166]

She obliged, and within six months Kerkorian had a commercial pilot's license and a job as a flight instructor. But life as a teacher bored him. "I heard about the Royal Air Force flying out of Montreal, Canada, and I went up there, and I got hired right away," he recalled. "They were paying money I couldn't believe, $1,000 a trip,"[167] wrote Dial Torgenson in the 1974 biography *Kerkorian: An American Success Story.*

FLIGHTS FROM MONTREAL TO SCOTLAND

Kerkorian took a job as a transport pilot with the RAF Air Transport Command. He was required to fly Canadian-built de Havilland Mosquito bombers from Labrador to Scotland. Only one in four made it. The problem was twofold: The distance to Scotland was 2,200 miles but the Mosquito's fuel tanks carried fuel for only 1,400 miles, and only two routes were feasible, each more dangerous than the other. "The roundabout route was Montreal-Labrador-Greenland-Iceland-Scotland, but the plane's high-performance wings could be distorted by a paper-thin coating of ice, causing it to fall out of the sky. 'The snowfields and forests around that frozen perimeter were strewn with downed

231

Mosquitoes crushed like matchboxes,'" [168] wrote Torgerson.

He could fly directly across the Atlantic, riding a west-to-east air current described as the "Iceland Wave." Typically, it pushed Mosquitoes toward Europe at jet speeds, yet it wasn't always reliable. During mid-flight, if the Iceland Wave waned, plane and crew were in danger of crashing. During one Atlantic crossing in June 1944, the Iceland Wave lost all intensity. Next the sun set, then the reserve tank indicator pointed to empty, and Kerkorian prepared to ditch. But his navigator, knowing the plane would lose valuable altitude, begged Kerkorian to drop below the clouds to get a visual bearing. Fortunately, he went with the navigator's urging, and as they emerged through the bottom of the clouds, the lights of Prestwick, Scotland, twinkled ahead. Kerkorian made a perfect landing.

33 FLIGHTS EARNED KERKORIAN HIS SEED MONEY

During 2.5 years with the RAF, Kerkorian delivered 33 planes, traveled to four continents, and managed to save most of his generous salary, which became the foundation of his future wealth. In July 1945 after completing his RAF service, Kerkorian made his first visit to Las Vegas. He paid $5,000 for a single-engine Cessna, which he used for flying charters—which grew into a successful business.

During the late 1940s and 1950s, shooting dice engaged his leisure time, and he became well known as a Las Vegas high roller, nicknamed "the Perry Como of the craps table," for the mild-mannered way he won—or more frequently lost—$30,000 to $40,000 a night. Eventually, he quit gambling entirely.

Married three times, Kerkorian's most enduring union—from 1954 to 1984—was to Jean Maree Hardy, his second wife.

They met and fell in love while Miss Hardy was choreographing a performance at the Thunderbird in Las Vegas. They had two daughters, Tracy and Linda, whose names Kerkorian combined for naming his massive holding company, Tracinda Corporation.

In 1947, Kerkorian purchased a small charter line, Los Angeles Air Service, for $60,000, which flew gamblers from Los Angeles to Las Vegas. He later changed the name to Trans International Airlines (TIA), and offered the first jet service on a nonscheduled airline. That same year, he took out a loan to buy war surplus bombers. With airplane fuel in short supply, he shrewdly sold the fuel from the plane's tanks, paid off the loan, and subsequently owned the planes free and clear. Kerkorian operated the charter airline until 1968, when he sold it for $104 million to the Transamerica Corporation, receiving as part of the selling price, $85 million in stock. This made him TIA's largest shareholder.

In 1962, Kerkorian made a land deal *Fortune* magazine called "one of the most successful land speculations in Las Vegas' history." He purchased 80 acres on the Strip across from the Flamingo Hotel for $960,000. The $12,000-an-acre price was low even then, given that a narrow strip of land cut the 80 acres off from the Strip. Landlocked, "we traded the owners four or five acres for all of this thin strip that they could never build on," Kerkorian said. "Then I got a call from Jay Sarno, the principal owner of Caesars Palace, and that's how Caesars got started."[169]

By 1968, Kerkorian had already collected $4 million leasing the land to Caesars Palace, which eventually purchased the 80-acre parcel that year for $5 million. Altogether, Kerkorian grossed $9 million in the deal with Caesars Palace. Newly prosperous with the cash from the sale, along with his Transamerica stock, Kerkorian was primed to build his first Las Vegas casino resort.

ORIGINS OF THE INTERNATIONAL HOTEL

In the spring of 1967, Kerkorian purchased 82 acres along Paradise Road for $5 million. He hired architect Martin Stern Jr. and built the International Hotel,

which at the time was the largest hotel in the world. While the International was under construction, Kerkorian's business partner, Fred Benninger, suggested that because the International would be so large, they should purchase an existing casino-hotel and use it to train staff. The Flamingo Hotel and Casino fit their needs, was purchased, and became the training ground for the International. Benninger hired Sahara Hotel executive Alex Shoofey as Flamingo president. Shoofey then raided the best of the Sahara's top managers—33 in all—including veteran entertainment director Bill Miller and casino manager James Newman.

In February 1969, the Securities and Exchange Commission gave the approval for Kerkorian's International Leisure to offer the public about 17 percent of the corporation's stock at an initial price of $5 per share. Meanwhile, the Justice Department had acknowledged that gangster Meyer Lansky, Bugsy Siegel's cohort from the old days of Murder Inc., was a hidden co-owner in the Flamingo. Skimming the gross receipts was suspected, and more or less proven after Kerkorian acquired the infamous resort. The Flamingo reportedly never showed more than $400,000 in profits. However, in 1968, Kerkorian's first year, it earned a reported profit of about $3 million, because its alleged skimming operation had ended.

Later in 1971, Kerkorian sold the Flamingo to the Hilton Hotels Corporation. Regarding the International, "We opened that hotel with Barbra Streisand in the main showroom," said Kerkorian. "The rock musical 'Hair' was in the other showroom and the opening lounge act was Ike and Tina Turner. Elvis followed Barbra in the main showroom. I don't know of any hotel that went that big on entertainment. Streisand and Presley brought in some 4,200 customers (potential gamblers) every day for 30 days straight, breaking in the process all attendance records in the county's history." [170]

The location Kerkorian chose for the International was often criticized. Naysayers said that the 30-story, 1,512-room hotel was too big and too far away from the Strip. "We had the same doomsday people when we were building the MGM Grand, same people, same doomsday," said Kerkorian. "You have to ask a lot of questions and listen to people, but eventually, you have to go by your own instincts." [171]

THE ORIGINAL MGM GRAND HOTEL & CASINO

At the same time Kerkorian was making his initial imprint on Las Vegas, he became interested in the Hollywood film industry. In 1969 he began buying stock in the troubled MGM studios. By year's end he had acquired enough outstanding stock to control MGM, which he reorganized, merged, sold and resold over the years. From the MGM studio's acquisition emerged the theme for his next mega resort. On the 43-acre site first occupied by the Bonanza Hotel, in 1973, Kerkorian built the original MGM Grand Hotel & Casino, opening at that time as the world's largest hotel. Again, Martin Stern Jr. was the architect and Fred Benninger his partner. The resort had a movie theme to reflect

Kerkorian's interest in film making, and it offered many amenities and entertainment options, including jai alai, the fast-moving game of Basque origin. Visitors could engage in live para-mutual betting on the games as they were played.

The arrival of the MGM Grand as the Strip's first mega resort set a new standard for luxury and size in old Las Vegas, unmatched until the 1989 opening of Steve Wynn's Mirage. The resort also featured a large shopping arcade, a movie theater showing vintage MGM films, and eight restaurants—some named after famous movie stars, such as Tracy's, a tribute to the great actor Spencer Tracy. Of the MGM's two enormous theaters, the Ziegfield Stage showcased productions by famed choreographer Donn Arden, such as the long running *Hallelujah Hollywood* and *Jubilee*. The Celebrity Room showcased acts such as Barry Manilow, Dean Martin, Sammy Davis Jr., and Jerry Lewis.

On November 21, 1980, the MGM Grand suffered a disastrous fire. It started behind the walls of a first-floor restaurant and smoldered for hours before erupting into the casino and rising into the hotel. The fire killed 87 people, the worst disaster in Las Vegas history to date. The MGM Grand was refurbished in only eight months. It added another hotel tower and reopened in 1982. The MGM fire made such an impact that it instigated fire safety improvements worldwide.

Kerkorian sold the original MGM Grand, located at the southeast corner of Flamingo road and the Strip, to Bally's in 1986 along with MGM Reno, for a total of $594 million. The Las Vegas property was renamed Bally's Las Vegas, owned and operated today by Caesars Entertainment.

THE SECOND MGM GRAND

Kerkorian's next MGM Grand Hotel & Casino opened in December 1993. It was built on the old Marina Hotel and Tropicana Country Club site at the northeast corner of Tropicana Avenue and the Strip. Kerkorian again hired Martin Stern Jr. as the architect. Of course, his long-time partner Fred Benninger aided in the huge resort's development.

In the beginning, the intention was to develop the first true destination hotel in Las Vegas by including the MGM Grand Adventure Theme Park behind the casino. The notion at the time was to make the Las Vegas Strip more family friendly by developing attractions for children and young adults too young to be inside the casino. The resort was originally built with an extensive Wizard of Oz theme, featuring the green "Emerald City" color on the exterior and Wizard of Oz memorabilia decorating the inside. A yellow brick road completed the effect along with a statue likeness of Dorothy, the Scarecrow, the Tin Man, and the Cowardly Lion standing in front of the city. Besides the theme park, the resort featured a 380,000 square-foot convention facility, a 15,000-seat MGM Grand Garden Arena, the Grand Spa, 16 restaurants, numerous shops and night clubs, 5,005 rooms, and the largest casino in Clark County.

Although the resort proved successful, the theme park performed poorly and did not reopen for the 2001 season. The following December, MGM announced that the former theme park would be developed as a luxury condominium and hotel complex called "The Signature."

Three years later the MGM underwent extensive renovations. The Oz Casino was the first to go. In 1998 the main entrance on the Strip changed to a more traditional entrance. No longer would visitors enter through the mouth of a giant cartoon-like version of MGM's mascot, Leo the Lion. The reason: many Asian gamblers avoided the casino or used its back entrance because of the "feng shui" belief that entering the mouth of a lion brought bad luck. Instead, a large bronze statue of Leo was added above the Strip entrance to maintain the MGM lion theme. Leo's new statue stands on a 25-foot pedestal, is itself 45 feet tall, weighs 50 tons, and is the largest bronze statue in the U.S. Torgerson quotes Kerkorian saying he is "not a firm believer in the rule of needing 30 years of experience if you've got good, common sense." Kerkorian gave full credit to Fred Benninger for building the International, the old MGM, and the new MGM.

"I can't take much credit," he said, "except for seeing the big picture; the amount of rooms, what kind of showrooms, I'm into that part of it. But when you get into the nitty-gritty, I don't have the education to really get in there and dissect it." [172]

In May 2000, Kerkorian's MGM merged with Mirage Resorts, becoming the world's second largest gaming company, behind Harrah's Entertainment. In 2005, MGM Mirage acquired the Mandalay Bay properties, including many of Bill Bennett's projects under the Circus Circus name, such as the Luxor and the Excalibur. Among Kerkorian's many casino resorts are the MGM Grand Detroit, and the MGM Grand Macau which opened in December 2007.

In 2008, Kerkorian's net worth according to *Forbes* magazine was $16 billion, making him the world's 41st richest person. But by 2010, Kirk Kerkorian was among those hardest hit by the economic downturn, and as a result his net worth tumbled to a mere $3.1 billion. Not bad for someone who dropped out of school in the eighth grade, sold newspapers and earned a pilot's license by taking flying lessons in exchange for his shoveling cow dung.

STEVE WYNN: A VISION OF LUXURY

Similar to marvel entrepreneur Kerkorian, another innovative, self-made man accumulated wealth by developing huge, luxurious casino resorts in Southern Nevada—Steve Wynn. His first trip to Las Vegas with his family occurred when he was 10 years old.

Wynn once told an interviewer in 1983 that when he was young he'd go to bed at night and his father would sneak out to shoot dice at the Flamingo and the Sands. Wynn recalled that it was 1952, and to get to Las Vegas one rode horses through the desert and tied them to a hitching post at a casino's back door. "It was like stepping back into the frontier," Wynn said in a *Review-Journal* interview. "Casino owners were king; they owned the town. They were glamorous; they had beautiful women, and lots of money."[173] In time, Wynn's vivid observations about casino owners in 1952 would be made about Wynn himself.

WYNN'S EARLY CAREER

Growing up in the cold climate of Utica, NY, Steve Wynn

got his first gaming experience in a string of family-owned bingo parlors helping his father call bingo numbers on weekends. Wynn's father, Michael, tried to open a bingo parlor in Las Vegas, but was unable to obtain a license. He returned to Utica, and helped his mother, Zelma, to raise Steve and Kenneth, Steve's younger brother by 10 years.

Later, Steve took classes at Wharton Business School and on weekends continued helping his father run the bingo parlors. His father died in 1963, just before Wynn received a Bachelor of Arts degree in English Literature from the University of Pennsylvania. At the time of his death, Michael Wynn reportedly left $350,000 in gambling debts.

In 1963, Steve Wynn met Elaine Pascal, a hotel promoter from Miami, the daughter of one of his father's gambling buddies. Ironically, Elaine's father and Wynn's father earlier had joked about both their kids meeting and going on a date. Elaine was a blonde beauty, Miss Miami Beach, and at the time of their meeting attended UCLA. After they fell in love, Elaine transferred to George Washington University to be closer to Wynn. They married a few months after Michael Wynn died.

Steve Wynn took over the family's bingo operation and managed to accumulate enough money to pay off his father's debts and buy a small stake in the Frontier Hotel & Casino in Las Vegas. In 1967, he and Elaine moved to Las Vegas. Eventually he became the Frontier's keno and slot manager.

It was Wynn's investment in the Frontier that became perhaps the most controversial deal he ever made. The Frontier came with hidden owners, all of whom were mobsters engaged in the usual skimming activities. Had Wynn's associates been the

240

typical old timers out of the Prohibition-era roadhouses around Nevada, the gaming authorities might have paid little attention. However, within a year of Wynn's assuming his role of keno and slot manager, the gaming authorities pressured him to sell to a buyer they'd found, someone who could come in and clean up the place. He managed to avoid charges of wrongdoing when he sold his interest to billionaire Howard Hughes. Wynn later claimed he made no money on the Frontier deal.

No longer invested in the Frontier, Wynn got involved briefly in promoting lounge shows, and by 1968 obtained a valuable wine and liquor distributorship. He also made the most valuable contact any businessman could make in Las Vegas: banker E. Parry Thomas.

ENTER PARRY THOMAS, THE HELPFUL BANKER

Edward Parry Thomas, CEO of the Bank of Las Vegas (later becoming Valley Bank), was known at the time as the only banker in the country who would lend money to build casinos. Mainstream financial institutions thought casinos too devious to secure a loan. A shrewd banker, Thomas acquired a reputation for knowing more about southern Nevada real estate than anyone else. Robert Maheu, Howard Hughes' top aide, couldn't recall any major parcel of Las Vegas real estate Hughes acquired without consulting Thomas—including Hughes' six Vegas casinos.

One summer while the Thomas family vacationed in southern California, the banker moved into the Desert Inn so he could transact the deals Hughes needed done quickly. Thomas purchased properties in his own name for Hughes. In this secretive way the sellers didn't know that Hughes, the then-richest man in the world, was bidding for the property.

Thomas and the ambitious Steve Wynn immediately hit it off. Ultimately, Thomas not only loaned Wynn money to begin his casino empire, he also mentored the career of the innovative Ivy Leaguer. Wynn's wealth originated from a huge land deal he pulled off in 1971, which generated the seed money to ultimately make him a billionaire. It originated when he learned that Caesars Palace located on the busy corner of Las Vegas Boulevard and Flamingo road, was not the actual owner of a strip of land that ran along Flamingo. Howard Hughes owned it, and Hughes refused to

sell it to Caesars. As the *Review-Journal* reports, "But nobody knew more about the Hughes real estate holdings than did Wynn's new mentor, Parry Thomas, who had helped assemble them." [174]

Wynn found another site that Hughes needed, negotiated an option to buy it, then set up a trade with Hughes. Wynn was said to have snatched the Flamingo Road parcel from under Caesars' nose.

If that move wasn't clever enough, the next really was. "Wynn announced plans to build the world's narrowest casino thereon, forcing Caesars to buy the narrow strip for $2.25 million." [175] If Caesars had not paid Wynn for that narrow bit of land, the casino risked having a competitor located at their own front door.

Wynn and an undisclosed partner invested $1.2 million in the transaction, borrowing most of the funds from Thomas. When the deal was done, Wynn paid off Thomas, split the proceeds with his partner, and earned himself a profit of more than half-a-million dollars. This profit earned in the "Hughes-Caesars Land Swap and Sale" gave Wynn enough money to join with Thomas in what the *Review-Journal* called "the most famous bloodless coup in Las Vegas casino management."[176]

Once again, Thomas played an integral role in a second coup. Thomas informed Wynn that the Golden Nugget in downtown Las Vegas had one of the most desirable locations on Fremont Street. However, it was managed by a group of old-timers content with the status quo and not interested in making any changes. Thomas also informed Wynn that Golden Nugget stock was undervalued, and that the current operators didn't own much of it.

With this knowledge, Wynn and a new group of investors began buying up stock in the Golden Nugget until they had enough to get elected to the board of directors. In due course, they gained controlling interest. Next, they began documenting mismanagement, including employee thefts on the casino floor. That led to Wynn's calling for the Golden Nugget president, Buck Blaine, to resign. If he didn't resign, Wynn threatened to sue him.

"We can do it easy or we can do it hard," Wynn recalled saying in his confrontation with Blaine. "Bucky, sitting in that office of his, just caved in," wrote A.D. Hopkins in a *Review-Journal* article. Blaine bailed out with a $30,000-a-year tin parachute labeled a consulting fee.

By August 1973, Wynn ran the company, and in one year he increased pre-tax profits from $1.1 million to $4.2 million. To a Glitter Gulch that over the years had lost its glitter and much of its business to the emerging Las Vegas Strip, in 1977, Wynn added 579 rooms to the hotel, many of them the best Las Vegas then had to offer. Soon the Golden Nugget was making $12 million a year. As a result, not only did Wynn become the youngest casino owner in Las Vegas, but also the Nugget later received accolades earning its first four-diamond rating from Mobil Travel Guide.

By 1987, Wynn offered a total of 2,300 luxurious hotel rooms, which attracted new upscale clientele to downtown Las Vegas and made his empire enormously successful. In time, the Golden Nugget Las Vegas proved the foundation for Wynn's ultimate rise to prominence in the gaming industry.

THE GOLDEN NUGGET PARLAY

Once he transformed the Golden Nugget into the jewel of downtown, Steve Wynn looked to America's East Coast for more opportunities. In an old resort town along the South Jersey shore, gambling had just become legal. Though the old town had lost its tourist appeal, Atlantic City was still an interesting place. During its heyday, it had been a popular vacation spot, with its picturesque boardwalk, sandy beaches, and strategic location between two major cities, New York and Philadelphia. Wynn found an aging hotel, tore it down, and by 1980 had built another Golden Nugget with 506 rooms.

His next move really brought big-money players to both his Golden Nuggets. He paid $10 million for three years of "Frank Sinatra's silver voice and priceless image," which he featured in his showrooms and in the commercials for his casinos. The *Review-Journal* reported that Wynn "bought jets, helicopters and limousines to bring high-rollers there... raided competing casinos for proven casino employees, and lavished money to keep them.

By 1984 his net worth was estimated at $100 million."[177]

THE MIRAGE AND TREASURE ISLAND

In 1984 Steve Wynn sold the Nugget's Atlantic City property for $440 million, reportedly for a $230-million net profit, and used $60 million of it to further upgrade the Golden Nugget in downtown Las Vegas, adding the second hotel tower and showroom. In 1986, he used another portion of those proceeds to purchase a large tract on the Las Vegas Strip where it intersects with Spring Mountain Road across from the Desert Inn. This choice location had remained largely undeveloped but was not for sale, primarily because it was owned by the reclusive Howard Hughes. But after Hughes' death in 1976, those who ran his immense holdings began divesting parts of it.

At the same time as Wynn acquired the undeveloped tract he purchased two adjacent casinos from the Hughes estate, the Castaways and Silver Slipper. He developed the entire site into the Mirage, later adjacent to it he developed Treasure Island. At the opening of the Mirage in 1989, it became one of the most glamorous resort hotels in the world. It featured an erupting volcano, an indoor rain forest, and high-quality room appointments with an emphasis on service. The reported price tag to build the Mirage was $630 million, of which $565 million was raised by the sale of junk bonds issued by Michael Milken, nicknamed the "Junk Bond King."

Critics claimed that the lavish Mirage was an enormous gamble, given that junk bonds required payment of a high rate of interest. The hotel would have to make a million dollars a day to service the debt. In 1989, the *Review-Journal* noted that, "While it had 3,000 rooms to do it, nobody really knew if there was enough business to fill that many new rooms, particularly rooms that had to rent for more than the city average to pay the nut."[178]

Once again, despite the huge expense incurred, Wynn's endeavors in developing the Mirage proved enormously successful. His next resort project, adjacent to the Mirage, was Treasure Island Hotel and Casino. Built at a cost of $450 million, it opened in 1993 with 2,664 rooms and 220 suites. Nightly, pirate battles were staged in "Buccaneer Bay," an area in front of the casino entrance on the Strip. Inside, performing in the showroom was the first permanent *Cirque du Soleil* show in Las Vegas.

THE BELLAGIO

Inspired by the Lake Como resort of Bellagio in Northern Italy, Wynn expanded further on his vision of luxury, converting the razed Dunes' site into the elegant $1.6 billion Bellagio Las Vegas. This magnificent resort opened in 1998 with 3,993 rooms and approximately 10,000 employees. Its many features include a picturesque 8-acre lake with dancing fountains synchronized to music, an indoor conservatory, a museum-quality art gallery, and branches of high-end boutiques and restaurants from San Francisco, Paris, and New York City. The Bellagio's poker room was considered special by famed poker players. They referred to it as "The Office," owing to its high table limits. It included the high stakes Big Game that could usually be found in "Bobby's Room," named after poker great Bobby "the Owl" Baldwin, who became the Bellagio's first president under Steve Wynn. The Bellagio was credited with starting a new spree of luxurious mega resorts along the Las Vegas Strip. Among the more recent developments are Mandalay Bay, The Venetian, Paris Las Vegas, CityCenter, and the

Cosmopolitan.

In June 2000, the Golden Nugget Las Vegas, along with all of Steve Wynn's other properties, was purchased by Kirk Kerkorian. The consolidated corporation became known as MGM Mirage. To date, it is the second largest casino corporation in the world, after Harrahs Entertainment. The reported price paid to acquire selected Wynn properties: $6.6 billion.

WYNN LAS VEGAS AND ENCORE

Five weeks before closing the deal with Kerkorian, Steve Wynn purchased the historic Desert Inn and its adjoining golf course for $270 million. Then, with the net proceeds from his sale to Kerkorian, and with his ability to secure even greater financing, Steve Wynn took Wynn Resorts Limited public in 2002 with an initial stock offering.

Next, he built his most expensive resort to date, the Wynn Las Vegas, at a cost of $2.7 billion. The flagship property of Wynn Resorts is situated on 215 acres, across the Strip from the Fashion Show Mall. It has 45 floors, with 2,716 rooms that range in size from 640 square feet to villas of 7,000 square feet. This magnificent property opened in April 2005. Notably, one of its casino hosts is Joe Esposito, who was Elvis Presley's road manager, and best friend.

In the summer of 2008, hiring of employees commenced for Encore Las Vegas, Steve Wynn's most recent development in Sin City, modeled after the Wynn Las Vegas structure, although separate hotels both share the original Desert Inn site. Encore opened in December 2008 with 3,500 employees.

Abroad, Wynn successfully bid for one of three gaming

concessions opened in Macau, a Special Administrative Region off the coast of mainland China.

IS THE MOB STILL IN LAS VEGAS?

In the early years, it was suitcases filled with Mafia cash that financed the entrepreneurs who built Vegas's first casino resorts, such as Bugsy's Flamingo and Dalitz's Desert Inn. As the 1950s emerged, it was multi-millions in Teamster loans that fueled the massive building expansion of the fabulous Las Vegas Strip.

At the time Howard Hughes began his historic spending spree in Nevada, the cohort of underworld men who came to Las Vegas in the 1940s and 1950s were nearing retirement age. Las Vegans believe that Mob activity declined during Hughes' four years in Las Vegas, 1966 to 1970, partly because he bought out many of the old-timers when he purchased his six casinos, and partly because the authorities formed the Nevada Gaming Commission in 1955 to become more stringent in licensing, and the Feds turned up the heat when they instigated the Kefauver Hearings in 1950.

The *Las Vegas Review-Journal* included this observation: "Hughes' attorney, Dick Gray, pointed out to the Justice Department attorney that the FBI, Internal Revenue Service, and law enforcement agencies generally are very glad to see Hughes come in and acquire the gambling interests from less desirable owners. Just by showing up, Hughes changed Las Vegas forever. If one of the richest men in the world, one of the nation's largest defense contractors and a genuine national hero, was willing to invest in Las Vegas, it must not be such a sordid, evil place after all." [179]

Robert Maheu, who spent 13 years working for Hughes, said, "He cleaned up the image of Las Vegas. I have had the heads of large corporate entities tell me they would never have thought of coming here before Hughes came." All told, during the late 1960s and 1970s, some 14 publicly owned corporations bought into Nevada, purchasing 25 major casinos and generating nearly half the state's total gaming revenue.

The Nevada Legislature passed in 1967 and amended in 1969 several Gaming Acts allowing corporations to own casinos, which forever changed Las Vegas. It allowed publicly traded corporations to be registered as holders of gaming licenses, providing a broader base for investment in the gaming industry and giving Nevada that long-sought respectability.

Looking back, historians today generally believe it was Anthony Spilotro's street crimes that ultimately led to the demise of the Vegas Mafia. Once the authorities began investigating Spilotro's criminal activity, it was simply a matter of time before other Mob-related crimes came to the attention of police and the FBI.

In a final note, on December 1993 the original Flamingo Hotel structure was torn down and the hotel's garden was built on the site. Situated in the garden midst is a bronze plague set in front of the wedding chapel dedicated to Benjamin "Bugsy" Siegel. At the time the Bugsy Siegel Memorial was the only place in Las Vegas that formally acknowledged The Mob.

* * *

INDEX

Index

Index

Index

Index

Index

T

Index

* * *

ENDNOTES

[1] Hopkins, A.D. *Las Vegas Review-Journal*. The First 100 Persons.
Benny Binion.
Sleeper, Gary. *I'll Do My Own Damn Killin'*. Barricade Books, 2006.
P.2.
[3] Hopkins, A.D. *Las Vegas Review-Journal*. The First 100 Persons.
Benny Binion.

[18] Sleeper, Gary. *I'll Do My Own Damn Killin'*. Barricade Books, 2006. P. 35.

[19] Ibid. P. 37.

[20] Ibid. P. 42.

[21] Ibid. P. 44.

[22] Ibid. P. 46.

[23] Ibid. P. 159.

[24] Ibid. P. 194.

[25] Sleeper, Gary. *I'll Do My Own Damn Killin'*. Barricade Books, 2006. P. 223.

[26] Ibid. P. 223.

[27] Sleeper, Gary. *I'll Do My Own Damn Killin'*. Barricade Books, 2006. P. 224.

[28] Hopkins, A.D. *Las Vegas Review-Journal*, The First 100 Persons. Benny Binion.

[29] Kelley, Kitty. *His Way: The Unauthorized Biography of Frank Sinatra*. Bantam Books, 1986. P. 159.

[30] *Life* Magazine article, April 6, 1951.

[31] Reppetto, Thomas. *American Mafia; A History of Its Rise to Power*. P. 1.

[32] Maas, Peter. *The Valachi Papers*, 2003. Harper Paperbacks.

[33] Regan, Gary. *Book of Bourbon*. Seen on Rumrunners/Bootleggers, 2002, History Channel.

[34] Balboni, Alan. *Beyond the Mafia: Italian Americans and the Development of Las Vegas*. University of Nevada Press. 2006.

[35] Kelley, Kitty. *His Way: The Unauthorized Biography of Frank Sinatra*. Bantam Books, 1986. Unknown page.

[36] Fischer, Steve. *When The Mob Ran Vegas*. Berkline Press, 2005, P. 91.

[37] Holdorf, Bob. *Las Vegas Review-Journal* article. The First 100 Persons; Tony Cornero.

[38] Roemer, William F. Jr. *The Enforcer: Spilotro, Chicago's Man Over Las Vegas*. New York. Donald I. Fine, 1995. P.9.

[39] Fischer, Steve. *When The Mob Ran Vegas*. Berkline Press, 2005.

[40] Ibid. p. 45.

[41] Wilkerson, W. R., *The Man Who Invented Las Vegas*, Ciro's Books, 2000.

[42] Ibid. P. 9.

[43] Ibid. P 15.

[44] Ibid. P. 37.

[45] Ibid. P. 18.

[46] Ibid. P.16.

[47] Ibid. P. 38.

[48] Wilkerson, W. R. III, *The Man Who Invented Las Vegas*, Ciro's Books, 2000. Unknown page.

[49] *Las Vegas Review-Journal* Article: The First 100 Persons; Ben Siegel.

[50] Ibid. P. 110.

[51] Wilkerson, W. R. III, *The Man Who Invented Las Vegas*, Ciro's Books, 2000, P. 114.

[52] Bruno, Anthony. *Crime Library* online. Ben Siegel.

[53] *Las Vegas Review-Journal: The First 100 Persons*; Ben Siegel.

[54] Turner, Wallace. *Gambler's Money*. Riverside Press, 1965. Unknown page.

[55] Wilkerson, W. R. III, *The Man Who Invented Las Vegas*, Ciro's Books, 2000, P.115.

[56] Fischer, Steve. *When The Mob Ran Vegas*. Berkline Press, 2005, P. 8.

[57] Gribben, Mark. *The Myth of Mob Gallantry*. Crime Library online.

[58] Wilkerson, W. R. III, *The Man Who Invented Las Vegas*, Ciro's Books, 2000. P. 114.

[59] Ibid. p. 114

[60] Ibid. p. 115

[61] Ibid. p. iv.

[62] Ibid. p iv.

[63] Tereba, Tere. *Mickey Cohen: The Life and Crimes of L.A.'s Notorious Mobster.* P. 9.

[64] Ibid. P. 9.

[65] Gribben, Mark. Crime Online

[66] The Mob Attraction, an exhibit of Mickey Cohen at the Tropicana Hotel & Casino, Las Vegas, NV.

[67] Tereba, Tere. *Mickey Cohen: The Life and Crimes of L.A.'s Notorious Mobster.* ECW Press. 2012. P.

[68] Smith, John L, *Las Vegas Review-Journal article: The First 100 Persons.* Part II; Resorts Rising, Moe Dalitz.

[69] Ibid.

[70] Ibid.

[71] Ibid.

[72] A & E Television, *The Mob in Las Vegas*, 2000.

[73] Griffin, Dennis. *Battle For Las Vegas.* Huntington Press, 2006. Unknown page.

[74] Ibid.

[75] Brandt, Charles. *I Heard You Paint Houses.* Steerforth Press, 2005.

[76] Ibid.

[77] Knapp, George. "Detroit House Searched for Clues in Hoffa Case". Fox News. 1975-07-30.
http://www.foxnews.com/story/0,2933,121237,00.html.

[78] Roemer, William F. Jr. *Accardo: The Genuine Godfather.*

Unknown page.

[79] Russo, Guy. *The Outfit*. Bloomsbury USA, 2003. P. 2.

[80] Ibid. P. 2.

[81] Fischer, Steve. *When the Mob Ran Vegas*. Berkline Press. 2006. P. 139.

[82] Ibid. P. 136.

[83] O'Brien, Michael. *"The Exner File - Judith Campbell Exner, John F. Kennedy's Mistress"*, Washington Monthly, December 1999.

[84] Smith, John L. *Las Vegas Review-Journal* article, September 10, 2003. Marshall Caifano.

[85] Ibid.

[86] Rappleye, Charles and Ed Becker. *All American Mafioso —The Johnny Rosselli Story*. New York: Doubleday, 1991.

[87] Ibid.

[88] Pileggi, Nicholas. *Casino: Love and Honor in Las Vegas*. Pocket Books, 2011. P. 2

[89] Ibid. p. 24-25.

[90] Roemer, William F. Jr. The *Enforcer: Spilotro, Chicago's Man Over Las Vegas*. New York: Donald I. Fine, 1995.

[91] Ibid.

[92] O'Connor, Matt. *Chicago Tribune* article May 21, 2005. P.4.

[93] Weatherford, Mike. *Las Vegas Review-Journal* article. The First 100 Persons. Frank Sinatra.

[94] Ibid.

[95] Kelley, Kitty. *My Way: The Unauthorized Biography of Frank Sinatra*. Bantam Books. 1986.

[96] Fischer, Steve. *When the Mob Ran Vegas*. Berkline Press. 2006. P. 166.

[97] Kelley, Kitty. *My Way: The Unauthorized Biography of Frank Sinatra*. Bantam Books. 1986. P. 220.

[98] Ibid. P. 220

[99] Ibid. P. 266.

[100] Ibid.

[101] Ibid. P. 239.

[102] Ibid.

[103] Ibid.

[104] Ibid.

[105] Weatherford, Mike. *Las Vegas Review-Journal* article. The First 100 Persons. Frank Sinatra.

[106] Ibid.

[107] Ibid.

[108] Ibid.

[109] Kelley, Kitty. *My Way: The Unauthorized Biography of Frank Sinatra.* Bantam Books. 1986. P. 281.

[110] Ibid.

[111] Ibid.

[112] Weatherford, Mike. *Las Vegas Review-Journal* article. The First 100 Persons. Frank Sinatra.

[113] Ibid.

[114] Ibid.

[115] Ibid.

[116] Kelly, Kitty. *My Way: The Unauthorized Biography of Frank Sinatra.* Bantam Books. 1986.

[117] Ibid.

[118] Ibid.

[119] Ibid.

[120] Ibid.

[121] Clinton leads Sinatra tributes". *BBC News.* May 16, 1998.

[122] Kelley, Kitty. My Way:*The Unauthorized Biography of Frank Sinatra.* Bantam Books. 1986.

[123] Ibid.

[124] Guralnick, Peter. *Last Train to Memphis: Rise of Elvis Presley.* Abacus. 1995. P. 168.

[125] *Las Vegas Review-Journal* article. The First 100 Persons. Elvis Presley.

[126] Ibid.

[127] *Newsweek* magazine. Unknown author and date. Compiled

from *Las Vegas Review-Journal* article: The First 100 Persons; Elvis Presley.

[128] Ibid.

[129] Ibid.

[130] Guralnick, Peter. *Last Train to Memphis: Rise of Elvis Presley.* Abacus. 1995.

[131] *Las Vegas Review-Journal* article. The First 100 Persons. Elvis Presley

[132] Guralnick, Peter. *Last Train to Memphis: Rise of Elvis Presley.* Abacus. 1995.

[133] Ibid.

[134] Ibid.

[135] Tosches, Nick. *Dino: Living High in the Dirty Business of Dreams.* Vintage, London. 1999. P. 57.

[136] *Las Vegas Review-Journal* article. The First 100 Persons. Dean Martin.

[137] Ibid.

[138] Wikipedia online. Dean Martin.

[139] Freedland, Michael. *Dean Martin: King of the Road.* Robson Books Ltd. 2004.

[140] Smith, John L. *The Animal in Hollywood.* Barricade Books, 2004.

[141] Freedland, Michael. *Dean Martin: King of the Road.* Robson Books Ltd. 2004.

[142] Ibid.

[143] Ibid.

[144] Davis, Sammy Jr. *Yes I Can: The Story of Sammy Davis Jr.* Farrar, Straus & Giroux Inc. 1990.

[145] Ibid.

[146] Ibid.

[147] Ibid.

[148] Ibid.

[149] Ibid.

[150] Ibid.

[151] Ibid.

[152] Ibid.

[153] Ibid.

[154] Ibid.

[155] Ibid.

[156] Ibid.

[157] Maheu, Robert and Richard Hack. *Next to Hughes: Behind the Power and Tragic Downfall of Howard Hughes.* New York; Harper Collins. 1992.

[158] Ibid.

[159] *Las Vegas Review-Journal* article. The First 100 Persons. Howard Hughes.

[160] Maheu, Robert and Richard Hack. *Next to Hughes: Behind the Power and Tragic Downfall of Howard Hughes.* New York; Harper Collins. 1992.

[161] *Las Vegas Review-Journal* article. The First 100 Persons. Howard Hughes.

[162] Maheu, Robert and Richard Hack. *Next to Hughes: Behind the Power and Tragic Downfall of Howard Hughes.* New York; Harper Collins. 1992.

[163] Evans, K. J. *Las Vegas Review-Journal* article. The First 100 Persons. Kirk Kerkorian.

[164] Ibid.

[165] Ibid.

[166] Torgerson, Dial. *Kerkorian: An American Success Story.* 1974.

[167] Ibid.

[168] Ibid.

[169] *Las Vegas Review-Journal* article. The First 100 Persons. Kirk Kerkorian.

[170] Ibid.

[171] Ibid.

[172] Torgerson, Dial. *Kerkorian: An American Success Story.* 1974.

[173] *Las Vegas Review-Journal* article. The First 100 Persons. Steve Wynn.

[174] *Las Vegas Review-Journal* article. The First 100 Persons. Parry Thomas.

[175] Ibid.

[176] Hopkins, A.D. *Las Vegas Review-Journal* article. The First 100 Persons. Steve Wynn.

[177] Ibid.

[178] Ibid.

[179] Evans, K.J. *Las Vegas Review-Journal* article. The First 100 Persons. Howard Hughes.

* * *

BIBLIOGRAPHY

Balboni, Alan. *Beyond the Mafia: Italian Americans and the Development of Las Vegas.* University of Nevada Press, 2006.

Demaris, Ovid and Ed Reid. *Green Felt Jungle.* Buccaneer Books, 1963.

Edmonds, Andy. *Bugsy's Baby: The Secret Life of Mob Queen Virginia Hill.* Secaucus, New Jersey. Carol Publishing, 1993.

Fischer, Steve. *When the Mob Ran Vegas.* Berkline Press. 2006.

Hammer, Richard. *Playboy's Illustrated History of Organized Crime.* Playboy Press, 1975.

Hopkins, A.D., and K. J. Evans, editors. *The First 100: Portraits of the Men and Women Who Shaped Las Vegas.* Las Vegas, Nevada. Huntington Press, 1999.

Johnston, David. *Temples of Chance; How America Inc. Bought Out Murder Inc. to Win Control of the Casino Business.* Doubleday, 1992.

Kelley, Kitty. *His Way: The Unauthorized Biography of Frank Sinatra.* Bantam Books, 1986.

Lacey, Robert. *Little Man: Meyer Lansky and the Gangster Life.* Little Brown, 1991.

McLean, Andrew. *The Las Vegas Chronicles.* Scotline Press, 2012.

Pileggi, Nicholas. *Casino: Love and Honor in Las Vegas*. New York: Simon & Shuster, 1995.

Smith, John L. *Sharks in the Desert*. Barricade Books, 2005.

Turner, Wallace. *Gambler's Money*. Houghton Mifflin; 1965.

Wilkerson, W.R. III. *The Man Who Invented Las Vegas*. Beverly Hills, CA: Ciro's Books, 2000

Magazines and Newspapers

Chicago Tribune, Daily News. Esquire

Las Vegas Business Press. Las Vegas Review-Journal

Las Vegas Sun, Look, Los Angeles Times

Newsweek, New York Magazine

Internet

City of Las Vegas History, www.LasVegasNevada.gov.

Fremont Street Historical Facts, on-line site.

RECOMMENDED READING

Some of the stories in *Las Vegas —The Mob Years* are

updated versions taken from my 2012 book *The Las Vegas Chronicles; The Inside Story of Sin City, Celebrities, Special Players and Fascinating Casino Owners.* Also I read Havers, Richard. *Sinatra.* DK Publishing. 2004.

Regarding Las Vegas statistics, the author read articles by the Las Vegas Convention and Visitors Authority, State of Nevada Gaming Control Board, and McCarran International Airport.

PORTRAITS AND PHOTO CREDITS

Portraits by David Tomasovsky, Gulfport, Mississippi
Billy Wilkerson
Ava Gardner
Virginia Hill
Moe Dalitz
Benny Binion
E. Parry Thomas
Steve Wynn
Kirk Kerkorian
The Rat Pack mainstay: Frank, Dean, and Sammy
Howard Hughes
Tony Cornero
Johnny Rosselli
Elvis Presley
Frank Rosenthal

ABOUT THE AUTHOR

A former casino executive and 12-year resident of Las Vegas, Andrew McLean was a table games employee at the Flamingo, the Dunes, and Circus Circus. He's a graduate of Michigan State University, 1972, and along with his partner and soul mate, Liz Rouse, resides along the Gulf Coast of Mississippi.

Many of the stories in *Las Vegas—The Mob Years* are updated stories taken from his 2012 book, *The Las Vegas Chronicles* and his series of e-books titled *the Mob Chronicles. Episode 1; Bugsy* and *Episode 2; Benny Binion: Prelude To a Blood Feud.*

Mclean is also the bestselling lead author of *Investing in Real Estate* (6th Edition) and co-author with George H. Ross, Donald Trump's right-hand man in *Trump Strategies For Real Estate*; *Billionaire Lessons For the Small Investor*, published in four languages by John Wiley & Sons. McLean is also the author of several other books which follow:

Investing in Real Estate with Gary Eldred, 6th edition, John Wiley & Sons. 2009. Other translated versions available in Russian, Chinese, and Vietnamese.

Casino Player's Handbook: *The Ultimate Guide to Where and How to Play in America's Casinos.* 1998.

The Complete Guide to Real Estate Loans. John Wiley & Sons, 1983.

Making Money in Foreclosures: *How to Invest Profitably in Distressed Real Estate.* McGraw-Hill, 2007.

* * *